THE TAVISTOCK SEMINARS

Wilfred R. Bion
THE TAVISTOCK SEMINARS

Edited by
Francesca Bion

KARNAC
LONDON   NEW YORK

Appendix B, "Interview by Anthony G. Banet, Jr.", first appeared in *Group & Organization Studies* (Vol. 1, No. 3, September 1976, pp. 268–285), published by University Associates Inc. Every reasonable effort has been made to trace the copyright owners, but this has proven impossible. The publisher will be glad to receive information leading to more complete acknowledgement in subsequent printings of the book.

First published in 2005 by
H. Karnac (Books) Ltd.
6 Pembroke Buildings, London NW10 6RE

British Library Cataloguing in Publication Data

A C.I.P. for this book is available from the British Library

ISBN: 1-8775-344-8

10 9 8 7 6 5 4 3 2 1

Edited, designed, and produced by Communication Crafts

Printed in Great Britain by Hobbs the Printers, Totton, Hampshire

www.karnacbooks.com

CONTENTS

BION SEMINARS AT THE TAVISTOCK CLINIC

D uring the summers of 1976, 1977 and 1978 we spent some weeks in Europe, dividing the time between London, Italy and France. In 1979 we visited London twice—in March and again in September on our return from almost twelve years in California.

While in London on those occasions, Bion was asked to hold seminars at the Tavistock Clinic—fourteen in all. Unfortunately the few surviving video recordings came to light only recently and are of variable quality. Nevertheless, these survivals give a clear picture of the areas of analysis that were of major, continuing importance to him during the last four years of his life.

Transferring the recorded word to the printed page is by no means a straightforward process, especially if the speaker expresses his thoughts extempore (as Bion always did). At the same time, it is necessary to aim to retain the style and personal characteristics of his written work. Any changes I have made are in accordance with this aim.

Francesca Bion

THE TAVISTOCK SEMINARS

28 June 1976

[*This was the year of the record-breaking heatwave and drought. The videotape shows Bion wearing a short-sleeved, open-neck shirt rather than his usual long-sleeved shirt, bow-tie and jacket.*]

BION: It took me a very long time to realize that the actual experience of being psychoanalysed was a traumatic one and it takes a long while before one recovers from it. In physical medicine you usually have to go through a period of convalescence; you then hope that if you are fortunate you will reap some benefit from the violence that has been done to you physically. I was introduced to the kind of idea that violence is not done to you by psychoanalysis—that in the course of time you gradually got more and more cured. That doesn't seem to me to fit in at all; it was quite a long time before I began to feel that I knew where it was "at" and what sort of niche I occupied in this peculiar universe or domain that we call "psychoanalysis"—for want of a better word. But I can't say I have got very far with that particular line of thought. Part of the difficulty is that one has to borrow the terminology from all sorts of sciences, religions, aesthetic activities, in order to attempt to formulate a language of our own. There isn't

1

a suitable language for this extraordinary domain, but I am convinced that there *is* such a domain, that there really is something which it is fair to call a mind, or character, or personality. The problem is having to use a debased currency, a language that has lost a great deal of its value and has therefore lost its cutting edge—in so far as one has to use it for a particular purpose.

Freud described the situation in which people suffer from an amnesia—a gap, a space where there ought to be some sort of memory—and then fill this gap with paramnesias. That's fine, and a very profitable sort of idea it has been. But after a time when we get more and more accustomed to hearing about psychotherapy, psychoanalysis, the more we wonder whether there isn't another great gap—not amnesia—the vocabulary is so difficult we don't know what to call it. But anyway, when we are at a loss we invent something to fill the gap of our ignorance—this vast area of ignorance, of non-knowledge, in which we have to move. The more frightening the gap, the more terrifying it is to realize how utterly ignorant we are of even the most elementary and simplest requirements for survival, the more we are pressed from outside and inside to fill the gap. You can do that perfectly well—with art, with religion, you can multiply theory. You only have to ask yourself what you do individually in a situation where you feel completely lost; you are thankful to clutch hold of any system, anything whatever that is available on which to build a kind of structure. So from this point of view it seems to me that we could argue that the whole of psychoanalysis fills a long-felt want by being a vast Dionysiac system; since we don't know what is there, we invent these theories and build this glorious structure that has no foundation in fact—or the only fact in which it has any foundation is our complete ignorance, our lack of capacity.

However, we hope that it isn't completely unrelated to fact that psychoanalytic theories would remind you of real life at some point in the same way as a good novel or a good play would remind you of how human beings behave. Leonardo could draw things that remind you of what human beings look like. If you look at his drawings of hair and turbulent water in his Notebooks, there is an attempt to give an aesthetic representation of the sort of turmoil I have described.

Without wanting to forget all that—the fact of our ignorance and the fact that we have to try to make inroads into this universe in which we live by these various methods—scientific, religious, artistic—we can go on multiplying the number of approaches that we as individuals make, our own small contribution to scratching a little space into this great mass of material that we don't know.

I suppose it was permissible for biologists and others to talk about sex, but remember the furore that was created by Freud's suggestion that sex played a great part. The fact that he was able to do this also had the effect of making us see most of the development of psychoanalysis in terms of biological effect. Appropriate to that is the work of Mendel and his promulgation of the laws of inheritance. Of course, it begs the question when we talk about "Mendelian inheritance", because it is tautological. However, I think a rather awkward situation arises when it comes to supposing that there is such a thing as a mind, that we all have a mind or soul or psyche, or whatever you want to call it. We have to talk like that because we haven't a proper vocabulary for it. As soon as we recognize that, there is some gap there that isn't in fact quite empty. The borrowing from biology begins to break down when it comes to the question of the mind and the transmission of ideas. In fact, we have to consider that in addition to this biological inheritance, this Mendelian myth of propagation, it becomes one that applies to the world of ideas in which characteristics are transmitted from one generation to the next, or to some subsequent generation. We could say that on the one hand there are the genotypes, the genetic inheritance, and on the other the phenotypes, the transmission of appearances. I used to be taught to believe that these acquired characteristics are not transmitted—the only characteristics that are transmitted are the Mendelian ones, the genetic ones genetically transmitted. I don't think this is good enough; I think there is something quite unmistakable about the way in which *ideas* are transmitted. The individual gives birth, so to speak, to some other individual who bears signs or symptoms of these phenomenes—I am inventing a word to describe these particles that continue to be passed on, so that you can imagine a situation in which there is an English nation affected by Shakespeare and then the characteristics become, as it were, somehow transmitted—not altogether in an obvious way that you would suppose, by books and so forth. I remember John Rickman telling me about his experience at York railway station when a soldier came up to him and said, "Sir, weren't you at Northfield?" Rickman said he was. "It was the most extraordinary experience I ever had—just like being at university", said the soldier. That man hadn't a hope of ever getting to university—as far as we know. His educational and financial background, his cultural background, were all against him. So it was probably the only chance he had had. I don't know why, out of all the people at Northfield, that idea was transmitted to that particular person and changed his outlook—it certainly sounded as if it had. Whatever may have happened to all the pampered darlings of my generation at Oxford and Cambridge, they could pass through university without having the faintest idea of what a university was. But one man, who couldn't possibly know what a university was, almost certainly did. We are led to suppose that something happens to an individual, and then that "something" gets transmitted elsewhere; but the laws of Mendelian inheritance don't apply—some other laws do, such as phenotypes and phenomenes.

We can look at it very closely and in great detail, as in psychoanalysis. But I am not sure that the increased depth of observation that becomes possible when one is closely in contact with another person will tell us very much about this other form of transmission. Indeed, it is very difficult to know what effect an analysis has on the individual anyway. Some people certainly seem to be able to turn the experience to good account. But I think that in many cases it is purely ephemeral—there is apparently a "cure". We can use a term like "cure", but it has no lasting reality, no particular significance—in contrast with the basic, fundamental characteristics transmitted according to Mendelian laws. We could say, "That, Exhibit A, is a human being; that, Exhibit B, is a tiger, a cat, or a sheep." It would seem as if there are certain fundamental things that follow the laws of Mendelian inheritance. The other laws (if there are any) have to be discovered. It is possible that if you take a group of people—say, like those at Northfield—you might in the course of time be able to detect what sort of course is pursued there by an idea, by something that would seem to be a part of thinking. That is where people who observe groups may have a chance of seeing some of this form of inheritance.

To get back to the psychoanalytic view: it is quite useful to talk about "transference" and "countertransference". Or, as Winnicott puts it, the transitory object; it is in transition, in passage from goodness knows where to goodness knows what, from oblivion to amnesia—the tiny little bit in between that could be filled up by saying "transference relationship" and "countertransference", but I think it will have to be filled in with something else. Because the relationship of these little packets cannot be so easily determined, you may be able to see an idea zigzag its way through a group. I don't know where the idea comes from and I don't know where it goes to, but it may be observed *in passage*. This is where you get back to the practice of analysis and the practice of group observation.

Q: [*inaudible*]

BION: Pain is a fact of existence—not so very different from pleasure. Indeed I think that one requires a terminology in which there are not specific words so much as concrescences; a number of feelings or ideas get collected together and could be put into some sort of order. You could regard pleasure and pain as different ends of the spectrum.

It is quite easy to see why we like to have a nice feeling and even to believe that it is possible to have a nice feeling by itself. I think it is rubbish; you have to suppose that either you have feelings or you don't. If you are not willing to pay the price of the inescapable fact of pain, then you get reduced to a situation in which you try to isolate yourself. Physically it is quite possible: you can draw the blinds, turn off the light, have the telephone cut off, stop reading the newspapers and keep yourself in a situation of complete isolation—*physically*. Mentally, I don't think it is quite so easy. For example, even if it were possible to go back into the womb, it is very doubtful to imagine that one would be completely isolated so long as one continued to live. The human foetus lives in a fluid environment, the amniotic fluid, and embryologists say that it has these auditory and optic pits. At what point do they become functional? There is no reason why they shouldn't become functional, even to the foetus, because a watery fluid does transmit pressure. I think that, at some point, the foetus can be so subjected to these changing pressures that long before it changes from a watery fluid to a gaseous one—the air, birth—it does its best to be rid of the whole lot.

I think it would be a complete distortion of Kleinian theory to suggest that even a foetus might resort to splitting off thoughts and ideas and phantasies, and evacuating them into the amniotic fluid. However, I don't see why we shouldn't indulge in these phantasies. Freud said, "I learned to restrain speculative tendencies and to follow the forgotten words of my master, Charcot, to look at the same things again and again until they themselves began to speak" (*S.E.* 14, p. 22). I have great sympathy with that, but I think it is dangerous to imagine that we can do without these speculative adventures. Some sort of discipline is required.

It seems to me that if you consider what appears to be this curious progress from something like the fishy existence to the amphibian existence to the mammalian existence, there seem to be these archaic survivals. A surgeon will say, "I think there is a branchial cleft tumour." It's a survival, an archaic part of the body that proliferates and becomes dangerous. There's a vestigial tail, and that begins to produce a tumour and requires an operation. It would be nice, so seductive, if the mind, this archaic survival, could be so easily detected—but it can't. We don't seem to be able to smell it, touch it, feel it or see it, and yet we are aware of it. Unfortunately we can only say that perhaps we are completely mistaken: we are being stimulated by something or other, and then we build up this elaborate system of paramnesias, these elaborate systems of theory, because it is so much quicker, so much nicer to be able to fall back on theory. If I am right about this, then I think we could say that as far as mental life is concerned, we are in our infancy, we simply don't know what development is likely to take place or whether the development will be terminated by our magnificent equipment of simian capacity—being able to produce nuclear fission and blow ourselves off the earth before we can develop much further.

Q: [*inaudible*]

BION: Living in a watery medium, one of the foetus's long-distance probes is its sense of smell. Dogfish and mackerel can detect decaying matter at a considerable distance—in a watery medium. Transported to a gaseous medium, the individual carries a certain amount of the watery medium with it—mucous, saliva and so forth—and can therefore continue to smell things that are not completely desiccated; the watery medium that was once outside is now inside. Some people can be very sensitive to that; they don't congratulate themselves on their capacity to smell things that other people cannot, but complain bitterly of "nasal catarrh", talking exactly as if they feel afraid that they will be drowned by it. In short, this "catarrh" which could be an asset becomes a liability of which the individual is terrified.

I think this also applies to the eyes that show you things even if you are not in physical contact with them, and may indeed show you things that you don't like to see at all. . . . It is possible that we have hit on some measures by which we can develop our mental capacity. This is probably quite all right provided that it is more or less harmless. But suppose it becomes really penetrating; there is a mediaeval drawing of a person shoving his head through a sort of adamantine shell and is then able to observe the universe that lies outside. If astronomy actually enabled the individual to penetrate into space, then there might easily be an objection to that—a violent objection against all these radio telescopes and so forth, a wish to destroy them all because they made life so uncomfortable—it is so much nicer to be blind and deaf.

What it means, then, is this: are we going to dismiss X by saying, "Oh, he's terribly hypochondriacal"—finish; we thank God we don't have to bother any further? Or should we listen to what he says? Should we expose ourselves to what this individual is trying to communicate?

Freud said that we should pay attention to dreams. That has quite a history—lots of people have said it before, but Freud carried it to very great lengths, suggesting that we should have real respect for what we see and hear and experience when we are off our guard as we are when we go to sleep. There are very few individuals who have any respect whatsoever for the continuation of those dreams when they are wide awake. They are not even likely to admit to having them, because they know that the rest of us will call them hallucinations or delusions—as we all know, the authorities in some places are at pains to shut people up where they can do little harm—inside mental institutions. It is another future that lies before psychoanalysis likewise: to disturb the authorities and help them to imprison the human mind to keep it in a harmless condition. In a way we feel that it is all very well for people like Picasso or Solzhenitsyn—they were great men, and it was reasonable for them to put up with that sort of thing. But it is awkward to think that we, with our ordinary capacities, might have to stand up against it to support the movement towards freedom of mind, the movement that might aid development and discover the rules of mental nutrition. How do you feed the mind in such a way that it can develop, not get poisoned?

This is fairly easily discernible when it comes to a question of the application of drugs of one sort or another—alcohol, soporifics and so forth. But it is not so easy to know what *ideas* are soporific, what *ideas* are poisonous, and whether we, as analysts, are not furthering these developments of methods by which thought would become impossible.

André Green drew my attention to this statement: "*La réponse est le malheur de la question*" ["The answer is the disease, the misfortune, of the question": Maurice Blanchot (1907–2003), *L'Entretien Infini*]. In other words, the answer is the thing that will put a stop to curiosity better than anything. If anybody is at all curious, you can stuff an answer down their throat or into their ears and that will stop them doing any further thinking.

Q: [*inaudible*]

BION: The impression I get about morality is that it is basic. I have been struck by the fact that making a faintly disapproving noise will cause an infant to shrink back as if something very terrible has happened. I don't get the feeling that there is any conscious idea of what the crime is; in fact, the nearest that I have got to Melanie Klein's statement of it is, "free-floating anxiety". It is an anxiety without any concept attached to it—so much so that I think the growing creature does its best to find a crime to fit the feeling. So there is no difficulty about rationalization, no difficulty about having rational feelings for regarding someone as a criminal or thinking of oneself as one. And if the worst comes to the worst, the person can always commit a crime to match the feeling, so that the morality will actually precipitate the crime as a kind of therapeutic attempt; the person concerned can feel, "Yes, I may feel guilty, but who wouldn't? Look what I have done." In reality, I think that someone can really commit a murder in order to be able to feel that at least his murderous feelings of guilt are rational. But all this usually means is that the so-called rational event is one that we are capable of understanding according to our logical rules. That is a matter of our human limitations—it has nothing to do with the universe in which we live. Another trouble is the sense of guilt that can be so enormous that the person concerned tries to get rid of it, tries to embrace a sort of theory or idea that is absolutely amoral.

Q: [*inaudible*]

BION: Nearly everybody has been taught to bother about other people, to be concerned for them. That can also be one of these tricks learnt in the course of one's life—how to be *just like* a loving or affectionate person takes the place of *becoming* one. That is one of the solutions that put a stop to growth and development.

In analysis you have to be sensitive to the situation where the patient is talking very clearly, very comprehensibly, about his concerns for this or that cause or institution. In crude situations it is fairly easy to detect—yes, he is terribly concerned for the unfortunate people in—somewhere quite a long way away (there is no danger of having to do anything). So you begin to be suspicious that he is being just like a concerned person, just like a doctor, just like an analyst—and so forth through the list. But at some point it can become clear to you that a change has taken place: the patient is, in fact, bothered by something he *can* do something about. Then it becomes important to be able to draw his attention to this: that while he is talking in the same way as yesterday, or last week or last year, it doesn't sound as if that is the case. Of course, you do not want to be flattering, but the patient is much more likely to believe that you are saying this to suggest some improvement.

Q: [*inaudible*]

BION: When, in the course of the analytic experience, a change takes place, then you can say, "I think you are now feeling that you *are* the father (or the mother)." That might appear to be quite plausible for a person of about twenty or forty, but it may be more difficult to see that a child of six or seven is really a mother—only prevented from being one biologically because she isn't sexually mature. But later development of mature sex and real maternal feelings can be felt to be precocious, out of phase; the child then hates these maternal feelings: there is no chance of her becoming a mother—she just has to go on living another ten, twelve, fifteen years before she has babies. So by the time the really maternal person has a baby, she will have dropped the fancy of being maternal and has become sick to death of it. The human individual is a very defective creature. The snag is that there is nobody who can do anything about it except ourselves.

Q: [*inaudible*]

BION: The individual has to live in his own body, and his body has to put up with having a mind living in it. So in a sense the analytic procedure, if effective, could bring these two into some sort of harmony with each other. I think it is fundamental that the person concerned should be able to be in good contact with himself—good contact in the sense of tolerant contact, but also in the sense of knowing just how horrible he thinks he is, or his feelings are, or what sort of person he is. There has to be some kind of tolerance between the two views that live together in the same body. It seems to me that that is a preliminary to being able to extend it outwards to a situation where, if you can tolerate yourself as a father or a mother, you might tolerate a mate who is not you, who might be the other parent. It becomes easier to find the father or the mother for your children as well as your husband or wife.

As I say, I think the first aspect of this is getting into contact with yourself, because so many years are spent in which the individual is "morally" trying to be better, trying not to be a naughty boy or a naughty girl—you can hardly say, "I'm trying not to be a horrible foetus." So in spite of these attempts to evacuate, to give birth to, all one's horrible characteristics so that one remains the ideal person, it is in fact necessary to get to a point where you can tolerate living with yourself as a preliminary to where you can tolerate living with somebody else who will enable you to become complete, enable you to fulfil the biological function where the unit has to be a couple.

Q: [*inaudible*]

BION: At Northfield, where we had a marvellous programme—a wonderful affair—you could see where everybody was at any hour of the day or night—provided you didn't go and have a look. I remember collecting some men who were on fatigues sweeping the wards; I said, "Come along, let's go and have a look." First of all, we went to the carpenters shop—that was closed. Then we went somewhere else—no, they were on fatigues, so that wasn't operative. There wasn't a single department in this marvellous programme that was in operation—not one.

The tendency is to cut out all these intermediate phases, get to the position of authority and then add the authority formed into a kind of hard shell; no idea can penetrate that authority, no idea can penetrate that shell formed around the personality, the group or the community. Nothing short of a revolution, nothing short of violence, will crack the shell and release the people within it. That is why I sometimes say that an institute is dead: it can always obey rules and procedures; it can be flexible, and the rules can be altered to accommodate to the growth within. But the institute is always composed of people—and there is the trouble: the shell can be so thick that they cannot develop inside it.

4 July 1977

B ION: I find it extremely dull having questions answered that I haven't asked. So I think it would be preferable if I give you a rough idea of what I propose to say, and then if you will ask any questions you care to. I don't say that I shall answer them, but I can usually find a few more questions to ask you—a natural development, because most questions cause a whole lot more to occur. We never seem to get to the point of an answer unless we look back on it and think we have apparently gathered some kind of experience in the meantime.

I feel disposed to consider this kind of work from the point of view of the analyst: I mean by that the person who is theoretically responsible for the conversation. I am thinking of Freud's constant reference to Charcot's insistence on observation—that seems to me to be the absolute essence of it: observation. But what are we observing? Even the language we use is not adequate for the sort of difficult job that we do. We have to use the word, "observation", as a kind of metaphor, an approximation. In *Paradise Lost*, Milton talks of the situation in which he cannot fall back on his eyes because he is blind; he says he hopes he will be able to "see and tell of things invisible to mortal sight". We cannot hope for that, but somehow we do observe things that are very often not observed in the ordinary course of social intercourse. It would be useful if we could formulate in our own minds what it is that we are observing; it is a question which crops up all the time if we are doing this kind of work. Therefore, it needs to be kept in constant repair. How would you formulate it if you were trying to convey it to somebody else? What form of words would you use? It is curious that we do, in fact, resort to words; it is probably partly because the ability to talk articulate language is our most recent acquisition. But, of course, we are having to borrow words that have been used and formulated for quite other purposes, when the kind of thing that we are wanting to use them for now wasn't even over the horizon.

Having become as clear as you can as to what in your own experience you are really observing—never mind the books or what you have been told or anything of that sort—and having agreed that what you are going to use is verbal articulate communication, then decide what words you propose to use and draw up your own individual vocabulary. The words we have to borrow are like coins worn so thin that we can't read the superscription on them; we don't know their denomination and we don't know their value. To change the metaphor: it is like a surgeon who has to sharpen his scalpels both before *and* during an operation.

If we cut down our vocabulary to a minimum, then I think there is some chance of finding our own way of using the words to which we are most accustomed. And there is also a chance that analysands will gradually learn how to speak the language we are speaking, whether it is English, French, Italian or whatever. If you go on using the same words with accuracy—*your* accuracy—the patient has a chance of understanding what the words mean. Take, for example, a word like "sex"; it is borrowed from biology and is used by us as if it really meant something. If we were simply dealing with anatomy and physiology, I think it would be possible to use that word fairly correctly. When it comes to using it in what one considers is a mental sphere—assuming that there is such a thing as a mind or a character or a personality—then it becomes quite a problem as to where a person "leaves off", what are his edges.

Freud speaks about the "impressive caesura of birth" [*Inhibitions, Symptoms and Anxiety, S.E.* 20], and it is true; I find that people are tremendously impressed by that word [birth] and, curiously enough, also by the word "death". Both of them, of no importance whatever, are inevitable. There is really nothing to be said about them, but they are so impressive. For instance, you will hear something like this: "Will you come and look after these people in this particular ward of the hospital—they are terminal cancer patients." Terminal cancer: you only have to think about it to realize what a ridiculous phrase it is. How do they know it is terminal? Terminal of what? What is it the end point of? And in any case, we are not really concerned with funeral arrangements or something of that nature. What we are concerned with are living people, and if there is a job to be done for making the lives of people in a particular ward bearable for such time as they have to live, then there is something to be done. That has nothing to do with "terminal cancer"; it has to do with making such life still to come, still left over, still "in the bank" so to speak, tolerable and available, and finding some method by which patients can be given a chance of getting onto that wavelength where you bother with what *can* be done and don't bother overmuch with what you can't do.

I sometimes think there is almost an occupational neurosis of analysts, because so much time is spent in finding out the various mistakes which are made—our faults, sins, crimes and so forth—that we forget it is a very unimportant part of the whole story. We no doubt want to know what we are bad at—it is quite useful to know that—but the really important thing to know is what part of it we are any good at. So even if you have a patient who is supposed to be in "terminal stages", what is he still good for? What would you do with geriatric patients?

At the other end of the scale, people say, "It's no good to psychoanalyse a child of two or three or five." I have even heard fantastic statements about not being able to do anything when "the fibres are not myelinated". The trouble with the myelinated fibres is that the person who has them is often so rigid, so structured, that you can't get another idea through their myelin. On the other hand, if you have a reasonably intelligent baby and quite early in the proceedings you put it on a potty, its non-myelinated bottom seems to know what to do and then proceeds to perform very adequately without any fuss or bother. Why that is, I don't know, but I think the infant must have a personality—and so must old people, however ill they may be, however convinced they are that they have reached their terminal position. If they have, there is no problem. But there *is* a problem in that little, tiny gap of whatever it is—days, weeks, months between that point and the point at which they no longer exist.

Once again, we have to get back to considering that we not only have an anatomy and physiology but also a mind. "Canst thou not minister to a mind diseased?"—the question asked by Macbeth referring to Lady Macbeth sleepwalking. The answer would presumably have to be something like, "Well, not at the moment, but in four hundred years come along again and I'll tell you what we can do." Similarly today: "Come along again in four hundred years and we'll give you an idea." But in the meantime, each one of us lives this very short, ephemeral existence in which we can possibly use this hypothetical "mind" I am talking about to contribute something to the general fund.

There does seem to be some kind of inheritance of ideas or character or personality. It is not very much good falling back on the ordinary, accepted rules of genetic inheritance; we have to reconsider whether these *acquired* characteristics are not, in fact, transmittable. Then comes this point of how we are to transmit them.

I would like to consider the patient you will see tomorrow. I have a great advantage because I know nothing whatsoever about it, so I am not so easily misled as you, who probably think that you saw or heard that patient today. But I suggest that while it has its advantages, it is also a bit of a nuisance because it stands in the way of the fact that the patient has gone on living and thinking and will not be the same patient tomorrow as today—or at the end of the session as at the beginning. This point is curiously difficult to grasp in the actual practice—and that is what I am trying to talk about here. I am not very interested in the theories of psychoanalysis or psychiatry or any other theories; the important point is what I call "the real thing", the practice of analysis, the practice of treatment, the practice of communication. The question which then arises is: how are you to speak to this patient, the one you have never seen before but are liable to think that you have because you saw him yesterday? The difficulty is this: when you are dealing with a mind or character, the boundaries are not so clearly marked as they appear to be when you are dealing with the anatomy or physiology.

To fall back again on established usage, we can talk about the past, about infancy: in infancy the patient felt such-and-such, had this-or-that trauma and it had this-or-that effect. That is very useful if you consider the patient as developing in a line: born–married–died, *hic iacet*, finished. But the patient you see tomorrow is not like that; you don't see somebody who is "born–married–died". It is very difficult indeed to see what goes on between the beginning of the session and the end of it. One reason for this is that the noise is so deafening, the information we are constantly bombarded with through our auditory apparatus is so deafening. You know so much about your history, so much about the patient's history, so much about psychoanalysis, medicine, physiology, music, painting and so on, that it is very difficult to detect this "thing" that we are really observing—or wanting to observe. That is one reason why I think it is easier to "forget" what you know and "forget" what you want, get rid of your desires, anticipations and also your memories so that there will be a chance of hearing these very faint sounds that are buried in this mass of noise. I imagine that even a new-born infant has to do this: when it opens its eyes and is suddenly presented with masses of facts by its optic apparatus, then there has to be some sort of selection. This also applies to us from our angle.

Freud pointed out how important it is not to indulge your imagination, to stick to facts. I entirely agree with that—and am constantly contradicting it. I say to people in a supervision, "Look—when you are with a patient you have to be careful what you say. I am sure you ought to give the correct interpretations, but not here—here, I would like you to give your imagination a bit of exercise. So, say anything, however silly, idiotic, stupid, unjustified it is. Then, after you have said it, we'll get onto another point— 'what is the evidence?'—and so on. But in the meantime, cut out all of that and concentrate on what you imagine—speculative imagination, speculative reason." I know the objection to it: it is said that you can imagine anything you like, and certainly reasons are so common that they spring up like brambles. If you are hunting for the Sleeping Beauty of Truth, the difficulty is to cut your way through all these brambles. But I only have to say, "Give your imagination rein", to be reasonably sure there will be silence for the rest of the hour—nobody dares to speak, because everybody believes there is a psychiatrist knocking around the place waiting to tell them the correct interpretation, or to do the correct thing—which is probably to shut them up in a mental hospital or bring them under restraint in some way or another. The result is that their imaginations atrophy and become what I would call "sterile".

When you have forgotten all that you can about your patient—who will do his best to remind you—then you may have a chance of penetrating this impressive caesura of knowledge, facts, and a chance of hearing these very small things that are so difficult to hear or see. In other words—falling back on a rather metaphorical use of language—give yourself a chance to observe the growth of a germ of an idea. That germ may look very odd indeed until it has taken shape as an idea that can be articulated.

I would be very glad if my patient used any language he could mobilize—if I were qualified to understand that language. For example, if I say to the patient, "Where did you go last night and what did you see?", he may be very anxious to insist that he went to bed and went to sleep. [See also Seminar 6.] I say, "I don't mind what you did with your body. Where did you go and what did you see?" Presumably a person who is a very good artist would be able to say, "I'll show you", and would put a line on a piece of paper around that idea, and then he could show it to me. If the person was musically gifted, he could even make black marks on paper and call them "crochet rests" or notes on the stave of music. To me, they don't mean a thing, but I am assured by some people that they can read a score; and when they say that, they mean they can hear the noises. Incredible, isn't it? That is the sort of thing we have to deal with—facts which are incredible. That is the fascination of this job; if one can get through to a fact, it takes a lot of believing—no fiction can touch it.

As I say, it would be very much to my advantage if I could understand music, but the patient is restricted by having to talk to a person who has a limited command of articulate speech. So he has to do a lot of work to tell me what he knows—namely, where he was last night and what he saw.

Q: [*inaudible*]

BION: From the point of view of the analyst, you have in front of you somebody whose anatomy and physiology can be quite important. You may think, "This patient looks ill", and if you think about it for a greater length of time you may be able to define in your own mind what you mean by "looking ill", what an "ill" person looks like. A good physician will say, "Ah, that patient has a cachectic flush", and then from that point he can interpret what that particular flush means. Physicians usually call these things "diagnoses", but in fact they are interpretations—interpretations of the information brought to them by their senses. What information is brought to your patients by *their* senses one doesn't know, but you can get an idea of what information is brought to you by *your* senses if those senses have a chance of seeing, hearing, smelling whatever it is that does present itself; and then you can try to transcend those senses to find their meaning, their origin.

Putting this very crudely: in an analytic situation there is the analyst, a patient and a third party who is watching—always. So there are three people anyhow; very often there are others, much more shadowy—relatives, husbands, wives, fathers, mothers, children. Those "objects"—I use the vague word deliberately—exert an influence. So I am aware of something I call "hearsay evidence", the evidence I hear said, and I rate that very low indeed. If I try to evaluate it, I could say that the evidence I get from my senses while the patient is with me is worth 99, and all the rest share the remaining 1 between them; it is of such a low order that it is hardly worth bothering with. I can hear all kinds of things the patient has heard about me, has been told or believes, but what I want to hear is something that is buried in all this noise.

Physicians and surgeons are quite used to considering the findings of the embryologists who think there are signs in the human body of vestiges of different kinds of life, like an amphibian stage. When it comes to the mind, I think it is something similar; what I want to notice, if possible, are the vestiges, the remnants that have succeeded in surviving in the mind of a particular person. Buried somewhere in all the noise that is brought to me by the senses of sight and hearing, and what the patient is saying, including masses and masses of theories of medicine, psychoanalysis, painting, music, there is a vestige of something that is still operative. So if the patient actually turns up and there are two people in the same room at the same time, then you have a chance of seeing what may be these very faint signs. And perhaps, after a time, they will begin to fall together and form a pattern, and the pattern itself will form in such a way that you may be able to translate the impression that you get into articulate speech. It is complicated because we would like at the same time to be able to say something the patient could understand—and that is very difficult. First of all, it is difficult to get clear what one understands oneself, because of having to fall back on a debased form of communication, so devalued that it is hard to sharpen up the words enough to give them some kind of meaning.

So while there are apparently only two bodies in the room, I think we have to go beyond that and detect this third—at least—detecting what *it* detects. The analyst is being analysed all the time by this third party. After a while, if you are fortunate, even the patient gets this third party brought home to him enough for him to be aware of its existence.

Q: I would like you to expand on what you mean by "at least" a third party.

BION: Freud says it is essential in an analysis to lay bare the Oedipal situation. There, he is falling back on a verbal transformation of a visual image of three parties. I don't think it is enough. People also talk about omniscience and omnipotence; when you do that, you have brought in still more parties. I don't think it is reasonable to give an interpretation unless you feel fairly convinced that *you*, at any rate, have evidence of the presence of this third party, and then fourth or fifth and so on.

Melanie Klein said that the infant splits up the object into fragments which are then evacuated; she described this as an "omnipotent phantasy". But there can be a situation in which the patient has got rid of, to the best of his ability, all the senses that are disagreeable or unpleasant. For my part, I feel that I have good reason to think that this process takes place even before birth; the patient could be said to have ideas of which he has *never been conscious*. Of course, that is hopelessly contradictory, but then I am having to use language when I'm awake—articulate language. I don't think that Freud, in talking about the interpretation of dreams, really considers the fact that the patient who has a dream had an experience in what I would consider a very different state of mind from that in which he is when he is awake. Therefore, the story that the patient tells you, consciously, is *his* version of what happened last night, but he doesn't really know. I think the theory of the conscious and unconscious—which is extremely useful and, like all these things, becomes a bit of a pest after a time because it gets in the way of being able to see other things that one doesn't know—stands in the way of one's own ignorance, so that there is very little chance of investigating this realm of ideas that have never been conscious and this state of mind that is not available when a person is talking to you with all his wits about him in broad daylight, and you are listening to him with all your wits about you. There is a difficulty in our being able to penetrate through to our own knowledge and experience of what is taking place, because of this kind of diaphragm, this caesura, we can't get past but which makes available impressions not usually available to us when we are fully conscious and wide awake. That is another reason why I think there is a lot to be said for considering what I have previously called beta- and alpha-elements, but those are not psychological, because I keep them for something I don't know and never will know; I am assuming some kind of physical counterpart. But when it does become conscious, then I think it becomes a somewhat fanciful, theoretical construct—speculative imagination, speculative reasons.

Q: Is the germ of an idea rooted in the patient, in the analyst or in the relationship?

BION: It is in the relationship, but I think it is very unsatisfactory to speak of it as the transference and countertransference because although they are useful theories they become obstructive. There is something that rapidly comes to exist when there are two people in the room—one of them wanting to be analysed and the other wanting to be an analyst. So the germ of an idea really belongs to both. Of course, it is tempting to say that even in physiological sex this should be true of the germination of a child. If the two people were two minds coming together—not just two physiological objects, male and female, having intercourse—then I think it is quite a different matter. Something different is born, literally and metaphorically, from what is born when it is just a question of two bodies coming together—a penis and a vagina. In the analysis, where there is not usually physical contact, something analogous to that takes place; ideas are born if they are given a chance. I have tried to tell people that no matter how difficult, how awkward, how obstructive your patient happens to be, there is one thing it is as well to realize, because as you realize it, it becomes more and more useful—that the best collaborator you are ever likely to get is not your supervisor, or your teacher, or whoever you go to for a second opinion, but your patient: you are going to get your real cooperation from this person who appears to be so hostile, so negative, so uncooperative. It is easy to be flooded with all this abuse and hostility, so much information that you cannot get beyond it. Conversely, particularly if you are tired, you get a rush of theories to the head; you reach a point where, while it sounds like articulate speech, it is in fact noise, jargon. It is not really fair to expect the patient to be able to unearth the meaning of the floods of psychoanalytic theories to which he is being subjected. It certainly is a collaboration between the two, and there is something fascinating about the analytic intercourse; between the two of them, they do seem to give birth to an idea, and possibly, if you are used to it, you can turn it into an interpretation or a verbal construction of some sort. Patients get better and better at it until, if the pair are fortunate, the analysis becomes redundant, unnecessary, and they can part and go their own ways.

I haven't had the experience of analysing somebody who has become a composer, but I see no reason why a patient should not find that he is, in fact, capable of being a composer or a painter. Those are things that might come about if the person concerned allows his ideas to germinate in the way they would. Unfortunately it is much more difficult than it sounds; it is extraordinary how much one has an itch to want the patient to say it in his own words. But it may not be his method of communication anyway—he ought to be learning to draw or paint or compose music. That is what makes the actual practice of analysis difficult: you are trying to listen and observe, but you may be observing it in the wrong spot.

If you do that, you don't observe where the germ is germinating in the patient because your mind is focused in the wrong direction.

Q: How would you recognize this process of the germination of an idea, the characteristics of it as distinct from the "noise" you are confronted with? Could you describe how you get a sense that that is happening?

BION: I think it is similar to binocular vision; there is a point of focus at which the vision unites with one's own mind. How that appears from one's own conscious view of the situation is difficult to say. You can begin to feel, "I think I know what he means", and after a time it grows and grows, and you get more and more sure that you are right in thinking that you know what he means, and then you can give your interpretation. That is putting it, as near as I can, into verbal communication when one is quite conscious. Freud talks about being in a state of "relaxed attention". I certainly think that is right, but I think it also implies forgetting these various theories, preconceptions and hopes so that there will be a chance of the point of focus declaring itself.

In your practice you will find yourself under pressure. You say whatever you have to say, and then there is an entirely new situation. You don't really know what is going on because it *is* an entirely new situation, things will not be the same. It is likely enough that the patient will say, "Why don't you *say* something?" Or if not the patient, the relatives—"Why don't you *do* something?" So you are always under pressure prematurely and precociously to produce your idea. Poor little thing! Pull it up by the roots and have a look at it—it hasn't got a chance. So you have to act as a sort of parent to the idea—protect it and give it a chance to grow in spite of these pressures; you have to be able to tolerate this state of ignorance. Coming towards the week-end break or some other break, you are under pressure to produce some sort of result. I say, "some sort of result", but what you are really hankering after is spectacular cure, something you could really notice, that could really be shown.

Q: How do you distinguish between there being a third person or voice present and other things that come into your mind? How do you sense whether it is a genuine third voice that you *and* the patient can hear?

BION: I think the sign that it is not right is the sense of anxiety, of being out of step, the feeling that things are not quite coming together. Tolstoy speaks of Prince Andrei saying, "That is sooth, accept it—that is sooth, accept it". There is a certain point, or at least uncertain point, at which one feels that something has clicked. But most of the time you have to tolerate this feeling of being out of phase, or its *not* being right. It is difficult to do because the moments of illumination are extremely rare and very few. I console myself with the thought that after one has seen a patient for, say, five or six years, there may possibly have been three moments of illumination—and three is enough. I am talking about proper illumination, the real thing. There are stacks and stacks of rational explanations, rationally accepted; there is no difficulty about that at all. There are millions of what one might call "correct" interpretations, but the illuminating situations are the ones that really do the work. If the two of them can stand it, they may last long enough for that to take place.

Q: Is the real growth of the mind something that is outside transference and countertransference, where memory and desire are in abeyance and the new idea, illumination, takes place in spite of the change of those?

BION: They are not always discernible in the direct relationship, but in the course of time they are. That is where there is such a thing as the inheritance of acquired characteristics. For example, nothing will quite undo the fact that Shakespeare existed. Even now very few people can read a Shakespeare play; we are dependent on expert actors to interpret the phrases, and then we can say we have "seen" *Twelfth Night*, or *Julius Caesar*, or *Macbeth*. In the USA, the BBC productions are spoken of very highly indeed; they say the actors are so wonderful. Seeing a production of a Shakespeare play is a stirring experience, but in reading one we ought to be cautious and not get too misled by the fact that we can read—that is not good enough. It is like saying that because we can see black and white marks on paper, we can therefore read music—we can't. So people who aspire to read a Shakespeare play ought to go into a certain amount of training for the purpose, and to have certain minimum conditions in which to read it.

Shakespeare wrote, "The raven himself is hoarse that croaks the fatal entrance of Duncan under my battlements" [*Macbeth*, I.v]. There is only one word that is at all long—battlements. Put the lot together and you get a phrase that does something to you today. Where that comes from, I don't know—I don't know what happens to these things. I am reminded of Milton's reference to Alpheus: "Return Alpheus, the dread voice is past . . ." ["Lycidas"] and so on. There he is using the simile of the river that goes underground and then bobs up again somewhere else. Where it comes up and what effect it may have, goodness knows. A wild phrase of that sort goes through the ages. In a sense we could say, "Well, most people in this country talk English, so it's a perfectly understandable explanation." Yes, I don't want to deny the perfectly simple, straightforward, obvious explanation. What *we* are concerned with are the other explanations—even wild ones—which may be nearer the truth. That would help to explain why this country could never be the same again after it had had a Shakespeare.

The point is much the same with regard to the individual. You are asked, "Who is that fellow?" You can't remember his name, nor can the person you are talking to. Then a bit later, or at another time, you find you know the name perfectly well. Ideas also track their course through the mind and the personality in this way and are very difficult to trace. These ideas that have never been conscious do seem to be floating around and do break through; they come up much later when the embryo or foetus is actually a sophisticated person. So it is difficult to keep track of even one's own ideas. I am sure that everyone is familiar with the situation in which you are pursuing a certain train of thought and you get derailed, or "derouted", by some upheaval—you "lose your train of thought" because there is an emergence of some obstruction that prevents you from proceeding along the same line.

Q: You made the point about the idea arising between the pair. What about the group—such as the one here?

BION: There are great advantages in a group. Compared with a narrative story all in a straight line from A to Z, a group is like having the entire alphabet spread out. In short, between the lot of us we ought to be able to mobilize or germinate an idea that would be difficult for any single individual to produce. For that reason there is a lot to be said for universities, institutions like this one, for example, although it is bound to be clumsy because we have to place them geographically—we have to say, "Meet at the Tavistock Centre", and in this way it is dependent on a geographical distribution. But the more widespread the actual members of a group can be, the greater the number of bases for thought there are. This is why I was so impressed when Rickman told me about the private soldier he met at York station who said that the experience at Northfield—the Northfield Experiment when Rickman and I were there—made him realize what a university was. I have often felt that that man, who had had no chance of education after the age of fourteen, knew what a university was, while I very much doubt whether I or many of my contemporaries at Oxford knew that, even when we left. You could get a swimming blue, a rugger blue, a third in classics, a first in Greats, and so on through the list, but all those are irrelevant compared with having learnt what a university is. We had plenty of mental nourishment—so much, indeed, that I think the main point escaped us.

Q: What exactly had he learnt that made him think he knew what a university was?

BION: I would be tempted to think that he hadn't learnt anything if he thought he had learnt it exactly. One of the difficulties about mathematics is that it gives the illusion of having learnt something "exactly". I think the Intuitionists are right in suggesting that there is a lot more to be learnt. It is surprising that a man as acute as Keynes, who produced a workable idea about economics that has lasted pretty well up to the present time, should have branched out on writing about the theory of probability. *We* ought to have a great deal more to say about probability than anybody. When we are dealing with speculative reasons and speculative imagination, our only justification is to say, "This is not an exact science, it is not exactly anything." We could say that that introduces a certainty, but in this particular area where there simply is not enough evidence to amount to a fact, we resort to probability—it is *probable* that such-and-such will happen—and we have to be content with that. We have to leave the certainties to other people, and when they have got tired of the certainties they will want to know a bit more about the probabilities.

Q: I am reminded of an experience I had for many years with a patient who is exceedingly accurate. He is very skilled with machines but not with people. Today he surprised me with the following: his wife went to the greengrocer and asked how many pounds of potatoes she should buy for a dinner party of twelve people. The patient was so annoyed with her for asking this question because in his opinion it could never be answered. When he left the room at the end of the session he said, "I don't understand—you say it was fifty minutes, but I'm sure it was only ten."

BION: We have become used to the idea that time and space can be measured; there are various instruments for doing this, from a watch to the 200-inch telescope on Mount Wilson, to a radio telescope with a very great baseline. These mechanical aids are very useful for our everyday purposes; how much they apply to the realms we are bordering on when we start doing analysis, I don't know. Melanie Klein said to me one day, "Even with the most profound analysis, we can only scratch the surface." She was about right. It may appear to be dogmatic if we try to express ourselves as precisely as possible, but it is not dogmatism we are wanting to express; we are simply trying to use the language with as much exactitude as we can, because it is easier for someone else to understand what is meant if we are fairly constant with the use of words—or, as I put it before, if the individual can learn our vocabulary.

Q: I have been thinking that when an experience is over—such as that of the soldier from Northfield, or that of analysis—we are left with an idea, an experience to reflect on in tranquillity, free from the "noise" you talk about. Perhaps the times when the analyst is absent during the analysis—week-ends, holidays—

are very important too. I would like to hear what you think about that.

BION: That is the most important thing about it—the actual germination of the idea. But I think this also applies *in* the analysis. People seem to talk frequently as if they thought that the human character or the actual person behaves logically and rationally, but when you look into the matter that really means the person behaves in a way comprehensible to the analyst—which is quite possible if they obey the laws of ordinary social intercourse, the laws of grammar, the laws of articulate speech. But the fact that something is comprehensible to a mere human being is no justification for believing that therefore the universe in which we exist obeys the laws of human grammar, reason or logic. We are, after all, ephemeral creatures living on an insignificant spot of earth that circles (according to the astronomers) round an ordinary star occupying a somewhat peripheral position in a particular nebula. So the idea that the universe obeys the laws in such a way that it becomes comprehensible to us is sheer nonsense; it seems to me to be an expression of omnipotence or omniscience. This is why it is so striking that the astronomers have now discovered black holes in which the ordinary laws of physics and chemistry don't apply; they have discovered two holes—two, to our knowledge, in the entire universe.

5 July 1977

Q : You referred yesterday to three points of illumination in an analysis of five years. I would like to ask what the analyst was doing in the meantime; I take it that he had to say something. The problem seems to be how to foster and not prevent the moment of illumination arriving.

BION: The simplest answer is, the analyst is analysing. But, of course, that is simply a general statement. When it comes to the details of it, it is a much more difficult question to answer. I remember being asked a long time ago, "Does the analyst ever do anything except talk?" I said, "Yes, he remains silent." I think there would be a lot to be said for scoring it in the same way that music is scored, where you have "rests" marked. You can even mark the rate at which it is to be played. In fact, each communication requires the appropriate amount of time, otherwise illumination cannot take place anyway.

Take a book that I found extremely illuminating—Matte Blanco's *The Unconscious as Infinite Sets*. It is a tough book to read; in fact, when you first take a look at it you think, "I haven't got time to read this kind of thing", because it is perfectly obvious that either it is an outflowing of more and more theory, or it really has a meaning, in which case one has to spend a great deal of time reading it. To give people an idea of the time required for reading a particular book, it would be helpful to indicate, for example, "120 pages an hour", or, "9 pages an hour".

The illumination, as I have called it, is a very rare event, but it is built up in the time spent beforehand that extends far beyond the areas of any analytic experience. Some people know a good deal about life already, and then they are in a position to understand. When I went into the army in the First World War, I struggled to learn drill and all that stuff, and I really thought I was a soldier by the time I had been gazetted as an officer. I discovered I didn't know the first thing about it, and the more I saw of action the more obvious it became to me that I knew very little about it indeed—and didn't at the end of it. I was jolly lucky to get out without having got killed through sheer ignorance.

So this whole matter of what goes on in the meantime requires a lot of discussion—much more than is possible here in three days. I hope to add a little more each time I talk to you. But by all means ask the question again; go on asking it. I am reminded of the quotation from Blanchot, told me by André Green: "*La réponse est le malheur de la question*" (which I translated, and he agreed with it, as "The answer is the disease, or misfortune, of the question"). [See also Seminar 1.] In other words, *that* is what kills curiosity. When you have the question answered, that's the end of your curiosity if it is allowed to happen too often. Unfortunately the whole of childhood is taken up by having questions answered—you learn quite early definitions like, "children should be seen and not heard", and are intelligent enough to learn early on to keep your mouth shut because of what you might get put into it if you open it.

Although it is easy to give a kind of mental answer like so many psychoanalytic interpretations, in fact it is much more difficult to say that there really does seem to be a sort of two-way traffic even with regard to thought. So the sort of mental nourishment to which one is subjected from an early age, and which one is very eager to lap up, then builds up a barricade against any sort of illumination whatever—unless, of course, you happen to be one of these pernicious creatures like me. I got a reputation even by the time I was eight as a joke because I was always asking so many questions; I had the answer pushed at me by what happened to the Elephant's Child who asked the crocodile questions [Rudyard Kipling, "The Elephant's Child"].

Q: I am wondering what you would do if an adult patient brought you some paintings rather than trying to use verbal communication to express his feelings.

BION: I would certainly do my best to look at them and be told anything about them that the patient could possibly tell me. It is a form of communication, and one needs to be able to listen to all that one is told, even when it happens to be a silent communication—even the "rests" should be listened to. When somebody has drawn a line around his communication, it is very useful to be able to look at it in such a way that one gathers from it what is meant. Let me exaggerate that: suppose you have a chance of looking at Leonardo's sketch of the Virgin Mary and the Infant John. An extremely gifted man is able "to see and tell of things invisible to mortal sight" [Milton, *Paradise Lost*, Bk. III]. This happens over and over again with religious pictures you can see at any time when you go into the National Gallery; the painter has seen something with the utmost vividness and has been able to transform it into a communication with oil, pigment and canvas.

If you were to show a dog a picture of a rabbit, after he had sniffed at it and found he couldn't eat it, he wouldn't be in any way interested. But show a dog a movie of a rabbit, and then he will get really excited—he sees the thing moving and wants to chase it; he translates what he sees into action. I can't show my patients movies; I have to resort to verbal communication, sometimes a verbal counterpart of a pictorial image, as I have just done with regard to this idea of the dog chasing the movie of a rabbit. That is an attempt, verbally, to describe a visual scene; it is typical of the kind of transformation one has to make.

Considering our meeting here: there must be a great many thoughts that we cannot see or that may not be expressed. But as far as all of us are concerned, it is useful if we can imagine that we can keep our minds receptive. I am thinking particularly of these wild ideas and stray thoughts that I consider to be floating around the place in search of a thinker. But, of course, it means that we have to be prepared to be receptive to the thought or idea, whatever form it takes and however wild it may be. I am not advocating what used to be known as "wild analysis"; I hope to come to that point again some time.

Valéry wrote: it is no good thinking that the poet is somebody who writes a poem in a night of delirium, a drunken stupor, a night of fever; the poet is the cold thinker, almost a mathematician, at the service of an affine dreamer [*"Ce n'est plus le délirant échevelé, celui qui écrit tout un poème dans une nuit de fièvre, c'est un froid savant, presque un algébriste, au service d'un rêveur affiné"*—Paul Ambroise Valéry (1871–1945)]. That is, this person, however cold, however much of the abstract thinker, has to be *at the service of* the dreamer.

Dreams do not obey the theories of Freud or anyone else. There are lots of them; there have been plenty of theories about dreams in the history of the human race. So we should not be too narrow-minded to a point at which we don't even admit the right of the dream to exist—dream in any sense of the word, literally or metaphorically. And if we want to be geometrical, then at least it should be an affine geometry—something that has an affinity with the dream.

When a patient. tells you that he doesn't dream, the really important question is, "Well, what *do* you do then?" He certainly does something, and if he says he slept soundly, it sounds very convincing, doesn't it? But how does he know he slept soundly? Who was awake? Or what was awake? Where did this idea of "sleeping soundly" come from? If it doesn't come from the patient, does it come from the analyst? After all, there are two people in the room in a psychoanalysis. Here we haven't two people; it is like having the whole of one person at all ages and at all times spread out in one room at one time.

I mention this particular point because I know that some people are interested in groups, but I wasn't thinking of that particularly; I was thinking of it as a way of considering a matter that puzzles me very much indeed. Where do these ideas come from when there are two people together in the room? There are plenty of theories about it—transference, countertransference—but I am not at all sure that the very usefulness of those theories hasn't indeed made them redundant, and that the whole subject can be opened up with far wider boundaries than would appear to be the case if one stuck religiously, dogmatically, in a bigoted frame of mind to the actual boundaries that are already laid down—supposedly by Freud, but not all. It is one of these situations that start as the possibility of freeing the mind of its chattels, but very rapidly become a shell, an exoskeleton. And then it is difficult for any sort of development to take place unless room has been left in the skeleton for the further development of the creature inside.

We are perpetually dealing with this difficulty. As we try to express or formulate our findings—as I am trying to do here—so we also excrete a kind of shell around them, a layer of knowledge that we can neither penetrate nor break out of. And very soon we get to the point of thinking, "Well, I don't want somebody to start arguing with me, because they may say something and I shall have to think again." It is much nicer to feel that we are establishing a kind of authority that can't be questioned and then is an impenetrable shell inside which we lie snugly and simply deteriorate.

Q: I would like to ask a question concerning O. I can understand that we can never know the O but can only become O. What kind of experience is that for the analyst or for the patient at the moment of illumination?

BION: I find it useful to suppose that there is something I don't know but would like to talk about; so I can represent it by an O, or a zero, or a nought, as a sort of place where something is, but that I am very unlikely ever to get to understanding. I can only go on from such knowledge as I have acquired and such capacity for gathering further knowledge that I have retained. To that extent, at any rate, I think one is a prisoner of the information one's senses bring—sense of touch, sight, hearing and so on. I don't think, though, that it is a good thing to suppose that there is nothing except what is open to our senses—that seems to me to verge on the ridiculous. I cannot imagine supposing that we, as human animals, have really reached the ultimate in knowledge or experience, or even development. It is possible that we have; it is possible that our simian ancestry is much too powerful for us, our simian capacity for learning tricks far exceeds our capacity for acquiring wisdom.

I would like to remind you of a quotation from Ecclesiasticus [38.24]: "Wisdom cometh to the learned man through opportunity for leisure". [Revised Standard (Ecumenical) Edition: "The wisdom of the scribe depends on the opportunity of leisure; and he who has little business may become wise."] I think the version in the New English Bible ["A scholar's wisdom comes of ample leisure; if a man is to be wise he must be relieved of other tasks"] is better; it makes it clearer. The person has to have undergone the discipline required for the acquiring of knowledge; *after* that, there is the possibility of wisdom. But even that is dependent on the opportunity for leisure. So there is everything to be said for making provision for leisure in which these wild ideas, these stupid ideas, these idiotic ideas can have a chance of germination, however much you may be persuaded that the result would be the birth of a monster. Most people are convinced that if they were to allow their minds to be free, they would say something really monstrous. It would be quite wrong to say, "No, no, that's not possible; it's bound to be something *worse*", because I don't think so. After all, the Nuremberg Rallies were very remarkable pieces of organization and achievement; there is no question whatsoever about their being highly intelligent people. Whether they were wise or not is another matter. I wonder if there is any other way of finding out except by opposing them—"Take arms against a sea of troubles and by opposing end them" [*Hamlet*, III.i].

In the *Baghavad Gita* there is a description of a debate between Krishna and Arjuna. Arjuna throws down his arms and says he will not fight; facing the enemy which includes many of his friends, many of the people he loves and admires, he is not going to fight them. Long before I even knew of the existence of the *Baghavad Gita*, I remember having a debate with three of my friends before battle. The question was, should we or should we not fight? Should we go to our commanding officer and say we were quitting, it was against our consciences? Out of the four of us, I was the only survivor in that action; I never knew a battle in which out of any three people one was not dead at the end of the action. It is extraordinary to think that that was the sort of price that had to be paid if one really had to "take arms". Or to put it another way, when it is a matter of the extremely efficient organization of the Nuremberg Rallies and what seemed to be the incredibly inept organization of the British army, navy and air force, I haven't the slightest doubt of the superiority of the organization of the Nuremberg Rallies or of the Prussian Guard and so on. It seems to me to be a matter of the differentiation between good and evil. I wonder how that matter is ever to be settled unless opposition is taken.

The advantage of talking about a matter of this kind is that it is possible to imagine that one could track an idea through a community in the way that a good doctor can be aware of the ramifications of the lymphatic system in order to detect the spread of tubercular disease. In the same way it might be possible to track the course of an idea in a group to find out how thoughts or ideas spread through a community.

With regard to these wild ideas—if one dares to harbour them—after a time something happens to them and they can emerge in such a way that you can give them a name like "speculative imagination", or "speculative reason"; you can put a tag on the thing. Or you can say that you feel "anxious" or "frightened" or "terrified"—a few simple words used as labels to tag on to a particular sensation or idea that you get.

Then again, you can comprehend it pictorially: "Return Alpheus, the dread voice is past that shrunk thy streams. . . ." [See Seminar 2.] Milton is describing the way in which the river flows underground and then bobs up again somewhere else; it becomes famous as being the same river that re-appears in extraordinarily different places.

Unfortunately we are educated so that we think we have read or been taught poems like "Lycidas". But once we think that, there is no chance of observing the astonishing performance of that Cambridge undergraduate who was able to put these thoughts and ideas that had emerged in him into such verbal form that we can even quote it now over three hundred years later. When you see today's patient tomorrow, who are you seeing? What are you in contact with? When or where or how was it born?

Q: Would you be prepared to say why a result of speculative reasoning or imagining sometimes seems to be ambiguous and sometimes confused?

BION: It depends partly on the answer and partly on who or what hears it. There is always this problem of the formulation of the statement, however it is done—whether by a painting or a piece of music or by articulate speech. There is also the problem of the receptor and whether that receptor is sufficiently mature to be able to tolerate information that is brought. For example, "*Les espaces infinis m'effraie*" [Pascal, *Pensées*, iii.206: "*Le silence éternel de ces espaces infinis m'effraie*"].* That statement very clearly expressed the terrifying nature of being aware of astronomical space. Because of the limitations of our ability to see, we don't much mind about astronomical space at the present time. We *do* get a bit sensitive and restive if the space to which attention is drawn happens to be the space that we ourselves occupy; we are already in possession of it, and we don't want to be disturbed by the invasion of forces or thoughts from somewhere else—either the past, the future or the present. There is always this tendency to build up a defensive mechanism so that our own system of architectonics will remain intact and cannot be invaded. So a shell develops like the dinosaur's armour that becomes so heavy it can't walk. Its armour appears to be a successful response against the stegosaurus, but between the two of them they end up by being extinct—unless, of course, we still have our mental dinosaurs.

To return to the problem of where ideas get to as they track their way, like Alpheus, unseen, unheard, unobserved: are we not sufficiently trained? Or haven't we the skill to invent a counterpart of the electron microscope and have to fall back on such senses and commonsense as we have because there is no apparatus? Even when we do have the apparatus that could make us more perceptive, once again we wrap the apparatus around ourselves. So when a patient goes for a consultation, the doctor says, "Right—X-ray please, electrocardiogram, blood count" and so forth, and off to the path lab they go. So we get to a stage in which the "answer" rests in the hands of a computer: shove in the test results and out pops the diagnosis. If that goes on long enough, with a bit of luck we shall not need minds at all; there will be no more trouble. "*La réponse est le malheur de la question*"—that's what will kill curiosity in the end. It is so harassing to hear, "Yes, I know. Yes, I know. Yes, I know" over and over and over again. It is a nervous tic, like "I mean to say" or "You know". It's not the unconscious; it's a sort of modern version of the unconscious, a kind of way of doing without an unconscious by having such an apparatus of mental bricks and mortar that you can build up this wall all the time—"Yes, I know",

"You know", "I mean to say". You can go on like that for ever because you just don't have to think, And if you are the analyst trying to say something to the patient, you've got your work cut out.

Widening the view a bit: "The last man through bolt the Menin Gate"—there was no Menin Gate. Or, "Build the wall up with our English dead"—another way of putting it. So you can keep a good supply of dead thoughts and dead phrases for blocking the holes, for preserving one's small stock of knowledge undisturbed.

With regard to the work of the astronomers, suppose we are being affected now by waves set up by the explosion of the Crab Nebula in 1054. If that sort of thing is said, one day astronomers will become extremely unpopular people because they will upset and frighten us. At present it is only doctors, psychoanalysts and suchlike who upset people by saying, "I think you need an operation", or "I think you might try analysis".

Q: I am increasingly aware that although you invited us to entertain wild thoughts, the response of people in the room has been very tame in the way that questions are phrased.

Bion: It is very difficult to give expression to the wild idea. If people can possibly bear to have a wild idea and allow it to germinate, then they might be able to put it into a form that made it more communicable. In *Finnegan's Wake* Joyce says that you would have to spend your life reading it to acquire the language or the capacity to understand it. I don't think anybody is likely to do that. But then you get this curious effect: perhaps in another fifty years people will be able to read *Finnegan's Wake*; what has happened to the wild ideas that are triggered but not expressed, we cannot tell. But they *are* communicated and you do get this extraordinary effect that, if it were purely physical, could be expressed by the laws of Mendelian inheritance. But nobody that I know of has expressed the laws of the inheritance of acquired knowledge, and yet I think it takes place.

The advantage of the point you have mentioned is that in a group of this kind, maybe we could see the sort of thing that you describe, but also see the way in which an idea tracks through the community, and from that regard it as a sort of model that gives us some idea of how an idea tracks through the mind of the individual, using this very small community which is the totality of the thoughts, ideas and feelings that appear to be bounded by the physical integument of the body.

[*No more of this seminar recorded; approximately one hour missing.*]

3 July 1978

M ATTI HARRIS: I don't think I need to introduce Doctor
Bion to most of you here. We are immensely privileged
and delighted that he is able to continue his series of
talks he gives around this time every year, giving us the opportunity to share his ongoing thinking and development—in so
far as we are able. I think he would like me to emphasize again
that he is utterly willing, and even eager, to be interrupted at
any moment by any questions however "wild" they may be (as
some people felt theirs were last time). Those of you who have
had this experience will know that you will always get an unex-
pected answer which may seem extremely enigmatic, but afterwards may be very illuminating—and sometimes incredibly
obvious.

BION: The problem that seems to me to be extremely important
and, I think, more important every day, is one of observation. I get
so sick and tired of hearing about the various different schools
of psychoanalysis and their great superiority to the other one—
whichever it is. The possibility of arguing about their various
merits is simply endless—as long as you don't anchor any of it to

39

facts. I don't know of any scientific work that is not based on observation; it is a great comfort, because if you can base it on observation, then you have something to go on that is as near to fact as you are likely to get in this extraordinary subject.

If an individual finds that he cannot see, then the chances are that he will use a stick that he waves about, prods the ground, and seems to rely upon it to give him information. He learns how to use it and appears to be able to diagnose or interpret what he gets from striking other objects or feeling that the ground is soft or sandy.

What kind of stick or instrument do we use when we are concerned with what is supposed to be the human mind in order to supply us with facts we might be able to interpret? Psychoanalysis is alleged to be one of them. Of course I went through the considerable training courses both in the old Tavistock and the Institute of Psychoanalysis, learning more and more theories I understood one needed to know. But long after I had completed my training course and had begun to recover from that traumatic experience, I really thought I began to get an impression of what it was all about. I don't think I am yet satisfied as to what that impression was or how I gathered it—that is one reason why I would like to continue debating the matter here. You may be able to throw some light on the subject of what it is that we are observing.

Q: You used the word "mind" just now. In some of your books you prefer to use "personality". I am very interested in that distinction.

Bion: It isn't really a distinction; it is due to the fact that I don't know what to call the "thing". Sometimes I call it the "personality", sometimes the "character". Freud talked about an "ego", an "id", a "superego"; we hear of "soul", "supersoul", "spirit". The French have a word, "sortilège"; I don't know how to translate it, but it comes very close to it. "How to translate it?" That is the trouble. I have no doubt about its existence, but I cannot think of a suitable term, even falling back on such English as I know. I'm glad you asked the question because it goes straight to the root of the matter.

How are we to get anywhere whatever in the direction of what has so far been called a "scientific view"? Freud seemed to think that he was making a scientific approach to this question of human personality. There is a great build-up of psychoanalytic literature, and a great build-up of argumentation about these various theories. But the theories continue to be elaborated, and there continue to be people who think they have had an experience they would like to communicate. Melanie Klein was one of them; Abraham another; Jung, Stekel, and many more. But suppose someone thought that music might be a way of exploring—that is one human activity that plays a great part; philosophy is another; mathematics another.

I had occasion not so long ago to talk to some rather distressed parents and a very distressed teacher; the child in question could not learn mathematics. There didn't seem to be much the matter with the child—quite intelligent, but an absolute b.f. when it came to mathematics. Very puzzling: "2 and 2 makes 4"; he could learn that by heart one day but had forgotten it the next. I asked the teacher, "You must be able to hear what he says about this." "Yes." "So, can you tell me what he says 2 and 2 *does* make? Obviously it doesn't make 4—that is something he has picked up from you and his school. But even so, he cannot grasp what it means, and forgets it." It turned out that the teacher didn't know what 2 and 2 meant to the child, so I said, "You had better listen to this boy doing mathematics and find out what *his* mathematics are, and what 2 and 2 does add up to." Then one could fall back on a basic fund of knowledge; I have forgotten what it was like to be asked what 2 and 2 make, or to divide 10 by 5, and so on, but this small boy (from what they told me, obviously intelligent) made extremely acute remarks. So there couldn't be anything wrong with his senses— what he hears, what he sees. The information his senses bring him doesn't seem to have anything wrong with it, any more than one could say that if a blind man trips up and falls over, there is something wrong with his stick.

Some people have difficulty in learning how to play the piano. Someone told me that he simply couldn't make head or tail of it; he did his exercises and so forth, but didn't really get anywhere. But later, when he had children of his own, he found that thanks to the piano exercises he was a first-rate wrist-wrestler. So the muscular development had paid off; you could at last see a very good reason for those early years of music lessons.

Not long after this the very same person began to feel rather pleased he had learnt the piano because he got pleasure out of the musical sounds he was able to make. So there was some kind of expansion, development, going on in his mind/character/personality; this curious facility for playing the piano was conveying something to him that had now begun to have a meaning.

It is something like that I feel about this matter of psychoanalysis and characters and personalities—even groups of people. For example, take us here: why or how has such a diverse mass of people come together at the same time and in the same place? Of course, that can be very easily explained—so easily that it is completely fallacious, just one of these bits of knowledge that are a frightful nuisance. Indeed, I feel that most people reach an age where they have so much knowledge that they can't penetrate through to the wisdom—it's a new kind of forest that you can't see for the trees: you can't see the wisdom for the knowledge. It is peculiarly harassing to listen to someone like that; it comes over in this way: "yes, I know", "yes, I know", "yes, I mean to say", "but you know . . .", "what I mean is . . .", and so on ad infinitum. Rather more harassing, because it appears to be slightly more meaningful, is the command of masses of psychoanalytic theory. The noise that those theories make is so great that you can hardly hear yourself think. I find it is then useful to be able to shut off one's awareness of what is going on so as to cut down the turmoil enough for some relevant fact to get through, something we could call "evidence" on which to base our judgement.

The great advantage of individual analysis is that you have the collaboration, if you are lucky, of the one person who really knows—the patient. I think it is fairly easy to see that it is likely that the patient knows what he feels, and knows what it feels like to have a particular feeling. For example, he is feeling "terrible", or "anxious". I don't find that very illuminating, but I feel the impulse to take it seriously because it seems to me that it is the sort of verbal formulation of what another person might say—he has a pain in his hand and "it hurts". If you are carrying out a physical examination, you say, "Where is this pain?" Or the patient shows you the place in his hand where it hurts, and you can continue your examination from there.

The kind of people I am talking about don't tell you "it hurts"; they say they are anxious or frightened. I am convinced that that is simply an approximation, an attempt to verbalize something not yet verbalized; that patient is suffering from pain.

Falling back on ordinary speech, as one has to, I have to say, "mental pain". I think it is a rotten expression, but it's the best I can do. It may get a bit clearer later on as to why I don't think it is good enough.

If the person in question is a painter, then he employs various shades of colour that are much more subtle. In fact, what he is doing is really exploiting light—and that is very near to becoming something that can be scientifically expressed in angstrom units and so forth. We are not so lucky as to have anything so precise— we have to put up with words like "anxious", "terrible", "frightened" or sometimes, "I had a terrible night last night. As a matter of fact we had a very good evening indeed." This last example is most effective because you are invited to pay no attention whatsoever to the fact that the patient said he had a terrible feeling. But when the patient enters the consulting-room, I regard myself as fortunate because he is so cooperative as to have taken the trouble to get there and present himself, and I am lucky enough to have a chance to observe this person who is not me.

The communication, whether it is what I can see or hear, presents me with what I now think of as "mental debris"—all this stuff that has accumulated between the time of birth and that particular morning; the stuff learnt in school, from parents, from the senses. I am not sure about this matter of when we were "born": I have no idea when the optic and auditory pits become functional; I have never heard anyone offer suggestions about that, but clearly, at some stage, there is a development taking place that makes available to the embryo or foetus what one day we could call "sensations", feelings, thoughts, ideas. Whether it is pressure of the amniotic fluid on the optic pits, or waves that are produced, I don't know. But I can see that in this sense the debris I am talking about can be a very considerable collection.

I can watch the patient, see him lie right on the edge of the couch, and wonder why on earth he does that. Why not lie comfortably in the middle of it? Why doesn't he say anything? Or why does he say, "yes, I know, yes, I know", ad infinitum? Why does he say he has no imagination, has dreams, or has no dreams?—and so on and on . . . I have to observe *all* of it just on the off-chance that somewhere amongst all this debris there is a scrap of information that is important.

I'm sorry not to be more precise than that—all I can say is that I still feel the need to be aware of this debris, not to allow myself to miss the chance of getting information in the hope that in my sieve-like mind I will catch up here and there with a piece of knowledge that is quite useful. Doing this sort of work fairly continuously and for a long time, perhaps one gets a bit more sensitive to these bits of significant debris.

I find the prospect of the patient coming to me for ten years, fifteen years, twenty years, somewhat unappealing—especially when he seems to be perfectly satisfied with the experience and the life he is leading but that appear to me to be disastrous. And yet, so much of medical practice—not just psychoanalytic but all the practice intended to be helpful to the human being—seems to me to lack discrimination, as if we had no way of being selective and don't know what to select. Unfortunately I think it is true. I have a better idea now, on the whole, of what I am likely to select, and I have a pretty good idea, too, since that is the case, that I long to be able to say, "Thus far and no further: what I don't know isn't knowledge", simply getting to a point where my defences, my resistance to any further information, will protect me from having to start thinking all over again. I try to resist that; one way is by regarding the patient I see at that session as an entirely new one. That is not so very wild, because time has passed and people get older; the patient you see today is *not* the same as the one you saw yesterday; nor is the one who started speaking a sentence still the same as the one who finishes it. It is a rather painful business; I find it very hard to resist falling back on what I already know about the patient, resisting having to think afresh, having to tackle the situation as if it is an entirely new one to which I have to bring a fresh mind.

To sum up: we are presented with the debris, the vestiges of what was once a patient and what still could be analogous to blowing on the dying embers of a fire so that some spark communicates itself to others; the fire is built up again, although it appeared to be nothing but dead ash. Can we look at all this debris and detect in it some little spark of life?

[*Tape sound faulty—section missing.*]

BION: Why does Newton engage on what I gather is a mathematical activity and start talking about life? And why does he similarly seem to encroach on what would appear to be a theological investigation? Why does Descartes find himself defending a theological position? The explanation he gives is quite simple: he does not like what happened to Galileo, and he doesn't want to get into the same difficulty. But his argument is not at all a good defence of that statement—in fact, it isn't a defence at all. It is quite clear that he is not intimidated by what has happened to Galileo. Over and over again there is this curious business of an inquiry, an investigation, followed by the link-up with what appears to be a theological theory or idea.

Freud talks about the future of an illusion [*S.E.* 21; see *Cogitations*, pp. 374, 378, 379]. I think it is quite an interesting speculation, but I would feel a bit happier if I knew which illusion, what future it is that one is investigating. Unfortunately, nowadays the collection of debris is very much increased by that of psychoanalysis. I don't think we hear quite so much about father-figures, but quite enough to get on with. Somewhere hidden amongst all this debris you can get a glimpse of actual suffering. It is rather difficult for analysts because we get almost hardened to human suffering—like doctors or surgeons who become so used to hearing about anxiety and so forth that they forget that it hurts. So we have to beware thinking that we are hearing about the real thing when what we are really hearing is the remnant of psychoanalysis. We cannot discard it on the grounds that it is simply a remnant (for the reasons I have already given). Therefore, we have to go through it all, whatever we are feeling like, on the off-chance that buried somewhere in this stuff is something that matters. And that brings me to the question I asked at the beginning—namely, what is this personality, mind or character?

If we could narrow it down and say what it is, then we might know what we are investigating and why we spend so much time and effort on this occupation. Of course, there are plenty of reasons that can be very easily arrived at, but I still feel there is a *real* reason, although there is a good deal of evidence to suggest that we tend to follow . . . [*break in recording*] under the impression that it is real illumination—cure, a good time coming, heaven, hell and so forth. So the seductive paths—what Shakespeare calls "the primrose way [that leads] to the everlasting bonfire" [*Macbeth*, III.iii]— are plenty, very effective and perpetually seducing us, or urging us in the wrong direction. The idea of "right direction" is curiously robust: the Chinese call it the Tao. Nearly all races of people at one time or another have stated that there is a Way, a correct path. So that is also worth further investigation when you get a view of it, perhaps in a patient who actually comes to you showing signs of thinking that there is some dread path from which he or she has strayed. Whether we can get this same idea from a group of people, or even a nation, I don't know. At the present time, people wonder why this country is in such difficulties. It seems to me that there are various, somewhat obvious explanations, such as if a country fights two Great Wars in succession, and is the only country to fight throughout both, then it is sure to have to pay for it in some way or other afterwards. [See also Seminar 8.] It is typical of the kind of question that plagues us; in fact, curiosity itself is a bit of a nuisance because it doesn't let us rest; it always leads to wanting to know more about something of which we know nothing.

Q: [*inaudible*]

BION: When we are awake I don't think we really know much about the state of mind in which we are when asleep. As a psychoanalyst I have been taught a good deal about the interpretation of dreams. The only thing I am not quite clear about is, what was the dream? Because when I am told that the patient has had a dream, it is told me by a person who is in an "awake" state of mind [see also Seminar 3]. I sometimes ask patients, "Where were you last night? What did you see? Where did you go?" I don't accept the answer that they didn't go anywhere, they simply went to bed and went to sleep. But I still think they went somewhere and saw something. It is possible that if the patient says he had a dream, it is a sort of vestige that is sufficiently robust still to be apparently available when he is awake. I find it very difficult to believe that the story he tells me is the current version of where he went and what he saw when he was in that other state of mind, partly because I have felt increasingly that there are occasions on which there is evidence of this state of mind when he was asleep. For example, the patient who lies on the extreme edge of the couch tells me that he dreamt he was sitting on the mantelpiece—some narrow ledge on which it would be impossible to sit. So there are these curious survivals into a state of mind when the person is awake, of events that occurred when he was asleep. At other times the patient appears to be awake and fully aware of much the same kind of circumstances as those of which I am aware in the consulting-room. As he goes on talking— it may be for as much as a month or so—I begin to feel there is a pattern about his behaviour that shows he is not experiencing the kind of events that I am experiencing. There are lots of words like "hallucinations", "delusions" and so on; they are very inadequate formulations because the experience I appear to be witnessing is much more subtle—so much so, indeed, that I couldn't very well give you a description of it.

I have had occasion to say to a patient, "You say that your paper on so-and-so has been rejected. I gather from what you say that it is a good paper. Why are you bothering about it being rejected? Surely, if it is a good description of an actual experience, people would be interested to hear of it." Some descriptions of the way that human beings behave seem to gather quite a lot of interest. If I were offered the choice of seeing how Shakespeare thought that human beings behave, or the chance of hearing a psychoanalyst's description of how a human being behaves, I think I would get a much better impression from Shakespeare. What he says reminds me of people; it makes me think that the sort of person he is talking about could possibly behave just like that. But most scientific papers don't throw me in that way; I don't look forward with a vast and vivid interest to the next edition of a learned journal, because I don't think it is going to remind me at all of how human beings behave or, indeed, of how I or other people I see for myself behave.

There is something about a patient coming into your consulting-room that makes you feel that behaviour is *about* something. The patient can say he doesn't want to come—he has come because he was sent. When he says he has just been sent, you can feel the untruth of that statement. It is not only the evidence of his actual physical, bodily presence—there is something else about it. Related to it is an experience you can have when the patient is said to be very idealistic, idealizes the analyst, and it is perfectly obvious that he does. But what is "perfectly obvious" is of no importance; what is important is what is behind that. If the patient finds that the universe he lives in isn't good enough and he has imaginatively to construct a better one, then what matters is *why* he has to construct a better one. Is it just sheer cussedness on his part? Or is there actually something wrong with the universe that we occupy? These are profound questions that have bothered the human race throughout history. When you get a little bit of history coming into your consulting-room trying to idealize you or some other person or analyst, the important thing about that is the force or drive leading to that idealization. The fact that it surfaces in the form of idealization may be a characteristic, but what really matters is "it"—the "reality". There is something about this part of the experience that could be called "real"—it produces a different feeling from "unreal".

I don't want to appear to be criticizing or running down my colleagues, but I have recently become more and more convinced that psychiatrists and psychoanalysts don't believe in mental suffering, and they don't believe in any treatment of it. In fact, they are living in a very precarious frame of mind, trying hard to believe in psychoanalysis—an awful effort and a continuous strain. Fundamentally they never get to the point of feeling that the person who comes to the consulting-room is actually suffering and that there is an approach to it that is on the right lines. Even psychoanalysis may be close enough to be on the right track, to be worth pursuing further. But not, "yes, I know".

It is a very curious thing indeed for an analyst with many years' experience to discover that his patient actually suffers pain. It opens up the questions: What are the dimensions of mental pain? Where does it hurt? Is it internal or external? Internal object or external object? All this is learnt so easily by intelligent people; a technical facility, very easily acquired, tends to produce a barrier against the real thing.

The experience of reality can be very unpleasant because it always carries with it the recognition of one's ignorance. You pick up a little bit of knowledge and wonder why you couldn't see it before, and what you are seeing now. So anything that you learn immediately makes you aware of the enormous area of the unknown and the incapacity to learn it.

Deflection from the path of learning is very seductive. You are likely to be misled because you are so pleased to be misled, with the result that even if you have a satisfactory experience you can doubt its validity. You can be pretty sure in any case that you would reach some satisfactory conclusion—the song the sirens sing is still audible to most of us; we are always invited to go off on some side issue as THE solution of all our troubles.

We are used to the difficulty of thinking clearly—a very feeble ability. Anybody who has the wit to arouse strong feelings can destroy your capacity to think clearly: if a patient threatens you with physical violence—either to himself or to you—it is very difficult to go on thinking clearly while going through that experience. The classical exaggeration of this is in war, where the fear for your actual existence can be so powerfully aroused that you cannot think clearly. In this respect a *real* soldier is different from an amateur, somebody who has not had a professional training or is not engaged in what is his natural profession. There is a great difference between that kind of person and one who is simply a temporary soldier.

[*Inaudible question*]

BION: I have great sympathy with the philosopher's aim to think clearly, and with his objection to anything that might endanger that capacity. But I also have a great respect for facts—even those I don't know.

With regard to objections to psychoanalysis or Mrs Klein's theories and so forth, I don't mind very much about people who don't believe in those theories. For one thing, I don't expect to hear them expressed adequately. Any formulation of a theory is really a crystallization of it; it doesn't leave room for mental growth or development—but it also provokes it.

An analyst should leave room for the growth of ideas that are being germinated in the analytic experience, even though the germ of an idea is going to displace him and his theories. I don't take the objections very seriously because Kleinian theories bear a great resemblance to sin: everybody is against them, but everybody practises them in secret. The secret of practice has a way of going on spreading, and if it is capable of development, so much the better as far as we are concerned.

I do sometimes wonder if the human race has reached the end of the road: its capacity for thinking clearly is just not adequate for the job that has to be done. If the astronomers are approximately correct in thinking they have discovered these black holes, for example, in which the laws (as we call them) of physics and chemistry may not be applicable, then the question is whether we are capable of finding any way of thinking or dealing with those situations.

Q: [*inaudible*] . . . the question of whether psychoanalysis can be killed, or a thought, once it has found a thinker, can be annihilated either in the individual or in the group.

BION: I think the individual can be annihilated; I don't see any particular reason for excluding the possibility that the human race could blow itself off the face of the earth, anyway. Technical ability has now become good enough to be able to produce really effective bombs. But I don't see how the truth (whatever it is) is going to be annihilated; I don't think it much matters whether we can grasp the truth or not. The laws of chemistry etcetera seem to me to be not of much higher status than the laws of grammar or English speech— very useful for purposes of verbal communication—but to suppose that the universe itself obeys the laws of English grammar seems to be entirely futile. And yet we very often behave as if there really were these laws that are something more than symptoms of our logical capacity.

The position of the formalist mathematicians, the logicians, is challenged by the Intuitionists—although what they say is very difficult for most of us to understand at all. But although we cannot understand it, or they may be wrong, they can be right in one respect—namely, that a purely logical construction does not go far enough, nor does an ability to *make* logical constructions, because the truth that has to be grasped can be far beyond our capacity.

However, the disposal of the human race is not really a matter of much concern; what does concern us is the extent to which we can live what remains of our capacity to exist in a manner that might be worth living. The capacity to think has so very few prizes to offer, in contrast to material possessions, that it is hard to get people to realize that there might be something to be said for thinking as being both enjoyable and useful.

4 July 1978

[*Only a limited part of this seminar was recorded.*]

B ION: That mobilization is something outside the group, the mobilization of the people who concentrate on the body, trying to keep the mind in its proper place. The development of the mind has been a frightful nuisance and has caused an awful lot of trouble. I think we are still frightened of it. That is why we [*inaudible*] . . . to what I call "wild thoughts", and anyone who will give a home to those thoughts flying around looking for a lodging, looking for a thinker to think them.

Q: [*inaudible*] . . . brought together two different concepts of yours—one, the beta-element, and the other the protomental apparatus. I don't quite see how they wed with one another [*inaudible*] . . . only for evacuation, and now you seem to be talking about them as manifesting themselves in somatic phenomena, habits and things of that sort.

BION: I invented the term with the idea that it could be vacant, a space "to let", as it were, that could be borrowed for purposes of clarifying something or another. But there are things that do seem to me to suggest this combination between the body and the mind. Why do the old anatomists call part of the brain the "rhinencephalon"? Why a nose brain? Why is a patient always complaining of a rhinitis? Psycho-somatic? Soma-psychotic? Take your choice. "Pure and eloquent blood spoke in her cheekes, and so distinctly wrought, that one might almost say, her body thought" [Donne, "The Second Anniversary"].

Some of the later developments of Confucius or his followers seem to suggest a sort of physical approach to what we regard as mental symptoms, mental diseases, and the suggestion seems to be of an athletic form of activity, as if they thought an approach had been made to these very primitive levels of mind via the body. When you think of this tendency, I think you will find with your own patients that sooner or later they have taken up dancing or gymnastics or eurythmics because of this need and urge to sweep athletic capacity into something that is so heavily concentrated in the direction of thought like psychoanalysis. Of course, it is very often done as a substitute for psychoanalysis, but not necessarily so—it may be a useful auxiliary.

Q: Bearing in mind the example you gave about the boy who could learn that 2 and 2 make 4 without understanding it [see Seminar 4], and the theoretical knowledge one can amass with internalizing it, converting it into wisdom, do you think it is inevitable that we have to go through a process of adding it on before we can reject the debris that isn't required? Is there any way round that? Do you have to amass it all before you can reject it and clear yourself?

BION: I haven't found any other way. Although I have plenty of reasons to be aware of the defects of the analytic approach, I can't think of anything better. The defects of psychoanalysis are bound to be painfully obvious both to the analyst and the analysand if you are at all sensitive to what is going on, but I don't know of any way of avoiding that. There is even danger in the educational system of supposing there is a way in which pain can be avoided. I don't think there is any way of teaching people mathematics or the piano or violin in such a way that the pupil does not think, "Right—when I've learnt this damn thing I will never do it again—I will never voluntarily submit myself to a musical or mathematical experience." That's hopeless; I would like the educational procedure to be of such a kind that a person might feel that he had learnt the violin because he would like to go on learning it. Otherwise, you get a position where the extremely gifted musician has a breakdown and concentrates on teaching the instrument rather than concert performances, fundamentally because of the rebellion against his own capacity—the better player he is, the more hostile he feels to a capacity that makes him spend all his life as a musician—or even a teacher. So I think there is everything to be said for not exaggerating what is in any case a painful procedure; learning anything new seems to be very painful.

Q: Could you say a bit more about people's rebellion against their capacities, talents, feeling that they become enslaved . . .

BION: I think it happens over things that are quite fundamental. For example, a child who is potentially maternal or paternal can be very alive to the fact that its mother or father is not treating a younger sibling wisely, but is quite unable to do better; if it is left in charge of the younger child, it does the job very badly. A person like that has to put up with many years of frustration before he or she has the chance to be a parent, and by that time they can hate anything whatever to do with what we nowadays call "sex", because they regard sex as having landed them in this trouble when they have sons and daughters. That seems to be against the very capacity to be maternal or paternal; it militates against the solution of the problem and contributes to the difficulty that arises in the course of any attempt to harmonize one's personality—how to get all the various impulses to live in peaceful harmony within oneself. The job of looking after that internal family is too much for the child. That is one reason why I think child analysis can be so extremely creative and can release these capacities in such a way that they can be harmonized.

Q: What is it that makes it possible to differentiate between "me" and "not-me" experiences?

BION: I don't know—and I am not at all satisfied with the attempt to talk about a soul, a personality, a supersoul, an id, an ego, a superego and so on. Those terms mean very, very little to me, and I find little that corresponds to them in my analytic experience. In the Society of Jesus, there is this idea of the "arbitrium": it is something that decides, has an executive function and represents the community of one's own interests or one's conflicting interests.

Cancer is one of these diseases that have a great appeal because of this quality of undifferentiated, undisciplined greed; there is only one way in which they agree, and that is to devour the body on which they are parasitic. But there are plenty of cancers that are not physical and that will in time become easier to detect in the sort of mind that is extremely skilful at mobilizing all its abilities concerned with "taking", in contrast to the sort of love that is "giving". The "taking" person will metaphorically bleed a group of all its life; that group will gradually succumb because of the presence of that person who takes the very life out of it.

5 July 1978

B ION: The difficulty in practice is this matter of scrutinizing what I have called conversationally—I would hate it to become a technical term—the debris. Perhaps what I mean by that may become clearer as I go on talking about it.

When the analysand comes into the room, is it possible to see the total situation, as it were, having denuded oneself as far as possible of one's preconceptions so that there is a chance of being aware of any facts that need to be observed? Although I am concerned fundamentally with talking to the patient, I am also concerned with the fact that he has a body and a mind. That division—body and mind—is convenient for conversational purposes, but it is a distortion of the facts because he is not "a body and a mind": I find it useful to think of a person as "your Self". But I would also like to make it clearer what I mean by "your Self" when I am wanting to stress either the somatic or the mental qualities.

Take this instance of the patient who appears to be perfectly fit and healthy, comes in, gets onto the couch and lies down. After a time you begin to notice that he hardly seems to disturb the covers on the couch; when he gets up and goes out, you don't have to smooth the covers—there has been hardly any movement. As you go on observing, a pattern begins to emerge (as Freud put it, quoting Charcot) and you notice that the patient lies precisely in exactly the same place. There is nothing remarkable about that, but when he lies in exactly the same place day after day, week after week, year after year, then I think you begin to be suspicious that he might just as well be lying on the edge of a precipice; from the amount of movement that he makes, he is lying in exactly the way that he might appear physically if he was in a cataleptic state.

It takes quite a long time before you see a point like that; it builds up over a period, and then you gradually see that there is something peculiar about it. The next thing you notice is that he says he has no dreams. In response to the question, "Where were you last night and what did you see?" he says, "You mean I had a dream?" Then what comes out is remarkably like a fact that you are acquainted with. Then you begin to think: this man is lying somewhere between what I am used to thinking of as the conscious and the unconscious; I think he is right—he doesn't dream. He is also right when he says he has no imagination. Whether he is telling me facts or whether he is telling me dreams—so-called—they are the same thing, a kind of mental counterpart of a cataleptic state. No wonder he makes no progress at all; the interpretations I give are based on ideas that some elements are conscious and some unconscious.

I had much the same sort of experience with another patient who was totally unfamiliar with, and apparently had no experience of, frustration—never been conscious of it, never been aware of it and therefore had no experience of it in the analytic sessions, never by any chance telling me what I might regard as a fact. I have no material to interpret, so I have to make a shift. I have to find a vertex from which these things will look different. So I begin to wonder what is wrong with this story: day after day this sort of behaviour, and apparently no progress at all and no objection to making no progress. It occurs to me that many of the interpretations I give could come over to the patient as being entirely obvious, as if I were simply repeating back to the patient what he has told me; the patient says, "Yesterday I went out and did some shopping", and I say, "Yes, yesterday you went out and did some shopping." So the question is, in what way is this story queer?

From that point of view, I can gradually shift onto a vertex from which it becomes clearer what the shape of this thing is. For example (this is something reported to me, not my experience), a patient had come for analysis for many years and then was admitted to hospital with an incurable cancer in the terminal stages. He asked to see the analyst and then blasted him for having completely failed to realize the seriousness of the condition he had always been talking about. Why did he want to see the analyst? Simply to have a chance of getting off his chest how much he hated the analysis, how much he hated the analyst and what a shocking piece of work he had done?

There is something very queer about this story. If it is true—and I don't doubt it—that this patient was in the terminal stages, you would think he would be concerned about how to spend such remaining hours or days, possibly weeks, of life in a way that was worth while. Why, then, does he actually ask to see the analyst simply to blast him in that way?

I suggested that the analyst should draw attention to this fact, because it seemed to me that this patient had never really dared to express the anger and frustration he felt; the nearest he had got to achieving that sense of freedom was with the analyst. It was no good expressing it to any of the hospital staff because they were concerned with telling the patient reassuring stories about the state of affairs and suggesting various forms of chemotherapy and so forth. I think this patient was longing for a chance of telling the analyst what he really felt and having the analyst speak the truth back again. The patient might have liked to hear just a faint dose of truth for once in a way before he died—a kind of last fling. That is what I mean by changing the vertex so as to see what was wrong with that story.

The analyst tried it out and was surprised and relieved to find that the patient began to talk of other things, including his dislike of the apparatus surrounding him—the apparatus that was intended to preserve his life but that went a very long way to making him extremely uncomfortable for such hours of life as he had left, and from a mental point of view was completely unconvincing. Nobody wants to be turned into a sort of nerve/muscle preparation to be kept alive simply in order to see the muscles twitch—and that is very nearly what was happening. The philosophical view behind it is that people need to have their lives preserved by whatever artificial means are available regardless of whether or not they want to go on living.

The patient who didn't tell me any facts at all didn't seem to lead any life whatever but was always telling me about somebody else and never experiencing frustration; he didn't have to because as the analyst I *did* feel frustrated. The explanation is so obvious that one feels a bit suspicious about it. I think it is a situation in which the patient is projecting part of himself into me so that I experience frustration but he does not. Nobody knows where that patient is—not even the patient. From that point of view, one could locate the frustration in the consulting-room if it was just frustration felt by oneself. But the location of the frustration was, in fact, faulty. Falling into it, having that experience and being the person who is made in various ways to feel frustrated while the patient is free of it is indeed a mysterious situation. One feels that there should really be some facts to support it—what are ordinarily called facts—but what *I* ordinarily call facts weren't there.

I know of no way of investigating this except analysis and having this kind of experience in which one can locate the presenting symptom. In this instance, it was my frustration. After I noticed this, and after I noticed that nothing ever happened to this patient, I realized that all these people he mentioned were parts of his Self. The only evidence I had was my own feelings, but the problem was, how does one communicate this to the patient?

I ultimately gave, with some misgivings, the interpretation: "I think you are making me feel frustrated instead of you, so that you don't have any feelings of frustration." His immediate response to that was a burst of anger and hostility. I said, "When I spoke to you just now, you were not aware that I had spoken to you; you reacted exactly as if you felt I had blown words into you that you did not want." In this way we did make quite a bit of progress: it became increasingly clear that the analytic situation was not simply a conversation between two human beings; that is what it would sound like, and anybody could be forgiven for thinking that was all it was, but it wasn't. This is not an infant or child; this is not an omnipotent phantasy of the kind described by Melanie Klein. I think her description of it ought to be retained because it is valid, but there has to be a distinction between that and the experience I am trying to describe. It is very difficult to describe it to anybody who hasn't actually experienced it, but quite unmistakable if you are participating in it.

I have learnt from this sort of thing that the evidence made available to you by any patient who actually turns up is far and away of greater consequence than anything you hear said—hearsay evidence, evidence the patient gives you about other people. When I have interpreted these facts—that so-and-so had written a letter, descriptions about the relationship of this patient with somebody else, but nothing whatever about the patient—that was really falling for it and treating hearsay evidence as being of real importance. I suppose it is of real importance with patients who are less disturbed, or with whose lesser degree of disturbance one is dealing, but I do put it in a very, very low category of analytic evidence.

Q: Is it possible that the situation you describe could be part of the unwanted self—the patient can't stand it coming back at him? Could it happen in cases where the patient feels there is nowhere to put that part safely outside and will then get attacked inside?

Bion: I think that does happen, but with some patients we have first to go through this stage I am describing. There is a peculiar reaction: the patient feels worse, and quite a number of people are drawn into the story wanting to interfere because he is so much worse. That is all outside the consulting-room, and I have no way of seeing how it is done. But I am sure that much the same methods are used as those I can see for myself in the consulting-room. In so far as the patient really does begin to take it back into himself, I think his resentment of analysis, of the analyst's interpretations, of himself for participating, does very much increase, and at that point so do the dangers of suicide. The patient is not so likely to make a physical assault on you—although I wouldn't rule it out, especially where lethal weapons are available—but he can make a lethal attack on himself. You can be called up: "Your patient is extremely ill; he hasn't eaten any food for at least five or six days." So you get an outbreak of what we used to call "acting-out". I am not quite sure now what I would describe as acting-out, partly because of the lack of any descriptive system of mental space. I *can* fall back on this when I am aware of the feeling of frustration contrasted with the patient who had none; there I can locate it and say, "Here it is." But when it stops and I am pursued with phone calls, interruptions and so on from elsewhere, then I cannot locate the places where it hurts. There still isn't a place where it hurts; the patient is not discommoded by having no food—the ambulance service might be if he fell down in the street and was found to be suffering from malnutrition, but in fact that hadn't happened.

I found out that the patient, who had been unable to get any employment for a long time, had found a job in a place where food was available and he *was* taking nourishment. It is very difficult to see why or how it was that everybody in the immediate surroundings had suddenly become aware of his malnutrition at the one time when he was getting food. I certainly think that there is a stage at which the resumption of the patient's murderous feelings is a dangerous one in the analysis, one in which he is likely to kill himself in one way or another. This particular patient was not killing himself, but I see no reason to exclude the possibility.

Q: Is the difficulty of shifting yourself from feeling that the usual things are not happening in the consulting-room, to being able to see that unusual things *are* happening, what you call "catastrophic change"?

BION: I think it is—yes. I am not sure in what way to approach this. One point is the difficulty of observing a change in analysis. I would now attribute it to the fact that I had not learnt that in analysis space has to be left for growth or development. I have to borrow these terms like "space has to be left" from ordinary language. I don't know what mental space is; I don't know any way of describing it, although I have given a paper [Los Angeles, 1975, unpublished] in which I talked about breaking up, breaking down, breaking through, breaking in, breaking out—take your choice. We hear people picking on one of them and complaining that they are "breaking down" or "breaking up". But the change of direction suggested when they begin to feel that they are "breaking through" is different.

Recently I had occasion to draw the attention of one or two people with analytic experience to the fact that they are beginning to believe that there really is such a thing as mental hurt. It is difficult to believe because verbal communications are carried out in a debased and devalued currency so that words like "anxiety", "embarrassment" and so on have very little meaning. Nobody really believes that they mean anything, but in the consulting-room "embarrassment" means mental pain. Sometimes you have to distinguish between different meanings of the same word; one that is commonly abused in this way is "sex", another is "love". "I had a lovely time", the patient says. You have to make up your mind as to whether the intonation with which it is said means that he had an experience in which he gained an enormous amount, or that at last he had an outlet to give something to somebody else. I think it is rare to find an analyst who believes both in mental pain and in the possibility of cure in the sense of some sort of genuine relief. Of course, the worst of it is that the word "cure" is virtually meaningless; if it has any meaning, it usually refers to something nice or pleasurable—not the ability to be aware of the universe in which one lives. The change I refer to is the kind of development that is not gradual nor something that takes place all at once, but rather jerkily. "I *see*", says the patient, and sometimes you feel that he does—he *has* seen something. It is quite different from "Yes, I know". When it is that degree of exaggeration, it is very easy to detect, but most of the time it isn't easy to detect nor is it easy to distinguish between these various intonations. A musician might be in a better position to do that, particularly a singer. I think any musician could probably get nearer to detecting these minute differences in tone. When I say "minute", I really do mean something very, very small.

This idea of the Grid: a classification to sort out one's own ideas about the kind of communications being made is pretty gross. You would have to reformulate the Grid to suit yourself in accordance with you own experience. It is just a kind of preliminary suggestion. If you could turn the Grid edgeways on, then it would become nearer to being a grating; the space between these various categories would get smaller and smaller and smaller. [See *Bion in New York and Sao Paulo*, pp. 91–92.] So if you could imagine looking at anxiety/fear in that way, then the space gets narrower and narrower, becomes just a chink, and what is a gross difference between anxiety and fear, becomes a very tiny difference. It is these minute differences we have to detect. And now the observation becomes a matter of having a very fine ear to hear, probably reinforced by what you see. Those are two extremely primitive developments in terms of optic pits and auditory pits in embryonic development.

Taking the embryologists' gross description that the human embryo goes through this fish stage of existence, the amphibious stage and so on, you can see what a change there would be in the relative power of the embryo's—observation? perception?—I don't know what to call it because these words have to be borrowed from ordinary conscious speech and ordinary waking life. But a sense of smell becomes a long-range perception; a primitive creature like a shark is able to smell food from a very long distance in a watery medium. What the embryo can hear and see also changes its character altogether; I haven't the faintest idea what to call it, but one day that person might turn up as a patient who was perpetually showing signs of something happening in the consulting-room without any explanation whatsoever. This sort of thing:

A. Well, what can I do for you?

P. But, doctor, I came here to find that out.

A. Yes, but I mean, what are you complaining of?

P. I thought you would tell me; I thought you would know what I was complaining of.

It becomes very clear after about the third question that you are on the wrong tack; it is no good pursuing that conversation any further.

What was that patient there for? Obviously you cannot know because you weren't there, but it would be surprising if it doesn't happen in your own consulting-room with one patient or another.

To take another example: I noticed after a long time—it took an awfully long time before I did notice it—that the patient was extremely sensitive to smell. I could detect this fairly easily; he arrived with all the essences of Arabia, and it seemed to be obvious that the smell he could not stand would be the one his untreated sense of smell could detect. After a time, such a patient begins to react at very short range; he is able to tell when he enters the room what is left over from the previous patient.

These same points apply to this matter of change in the emotional situation in the analysis. It is difficult when there is so much uproar of the past, of what you have seen in the patient before, so much evidence that you cannot detect the tiny changes until they have reached a striking proportion where the patient who couldn't work has started work (he may not have told you) and you are allowed to gather that by the smallest of possible hints, such as that he had difficulty in getting postage stamps. It is left to you to find out that he needed these stamps for a job he is doing—not just like that, but after several hours of work you can see it all adding up.

Q: Would the subtle signs that something is happening be in any way connected with the patient's fear of an unreceptive, rigid or hostile object that would object as soon as it began to feel that things were moving?

BION: It certainly plays a big part, because these patients are not only improved but are probably sensitive in a way that most people are not. The result is that they can become painfully aware of the reality or hostility and envy. Whether they are able to stand finding out what sort of universe they live in will depend on how robust they are. I use the word "universe" to mean anything from their private and immediate contacts to the society of which they are members.

I would like to say a bit more about that from a rather different approach—namely "vogue", meaning by that a very powerful force. It is not recognized as that because usually these fashions—subsidiaries of the same thing—are extremely ephemeral. But vogue is not; it is a very powerful characteristic, one that carries with it a pressure to conform to the prevalent fashion. It may sometimes be delayed: the fashions of today won't become general for, say, another year, and then they become commonplace. Psychoanalysis was all the fashion at one time; psychoanalytic terms were bandied about with the greatest of freedom by people who usually didn't know what they meant and wouldn't undergo the long discipline required to find out.

In the same way, you find that you can become a fashion yourself—you are under extreme pressure to act or behave as if you were a person of importance when you know perfectly well that you are not, and you know perfectly well that that fashion will change in a matter of hours, days or weeks. It is the vogue, and for the time being you are under its pressure. It then becomes clear that the honours are showered upon you in the hope that you will not emerge from deep under to the abuse levelled against you.

The group therapist should always be aware that from time to time, as the fashion goes around the group, *he* becomes the fashion, and his ideas or what he says are treated as if they are important. If you are not aware of that, you are liable to believe it yourself; the intensity of feeling can always be made to rise to a point at which you, the target, cease to be able to think clearly. The most obvious example of this is in war, where you hope to intimidate your enemy so much that he doesn't think clearly. It is not quite so dramatic or obvious in full peace-time, but it is nevertheless still there.

The big component in this is what I call vogue, the basic thing behind fashion, fashions in ideas. It is against that kind of pressure that the developing patient has to contend. Sometimes it becomes important to draw the patient's attention to it and say, "I think you are getting into a great deal of trouble because somebody is beginning to think that you are improving." When people become accustomed to the fact that somebody is neurotic or psychotic, they don't like having to change their views, because the person is now not quite so easily disposed of. Even a group—say of psychoanalysts, psychiatrists, psychiatric workers and so on—can always be in trouble if it is not possible to dismiss it as being a whole lot of crackpots. I don't think society would love us any more if it should turn out that, in fact, there are things we can contribute that it might not be possible for others to do.

These changes do seem to occur in little jerks—hardly perceptible, but adding up to quite a lot.

Q: Would you say that each little jerk has to break through something that resisted it?

BION: Yes, but it is very hard to know what that is. I am reminded of the fact that Picasso could paint on one side of a piece of glass in such a way that there appeared to be a different one on the other side. I saw an example of this in a child's drawing: the child had drawn a picture and told me it was a house and a tree. On the other side of the piece of paper was a meaningless scribble, but if I held that picture up to the light, then the meaningless scribble shone through the paper and the picture was quite different; it was somebody watering a plant.

As I said yesterday, it is interesting and important to know that a child cannot understand mathematics and why 2 and 4 make 4; but what one would like to know is, what *do* 2 and 2 make? In other words, look at the other side of this so-called resistance; look at the resistance in such a way that what is being resisted shines through it. When it is quite clear that it is analysis that is being resisted, what is shining through that?

From the example I gave of the patient dying of cancer in hospital, it seemed to me most unlikely that he would want to spend such few hours as he had left on just blasting somebody— unless, of course, he had never achieved the good fortune to be dying of a fatal complaint. So it isn't simply a matter of "changing the vertex"; it is also being able to see through the resistance or countertransference or whatever it is. All those terms are obviously very useful, but in many ways the analytic theories have been good enough to render themselves redundant. One seems to have to go through that process in order to make them redundant, to put them out of date, to put oneself out of date.

Q: I wonder if, implicit in what you are saying about the impact of change, in addition to his own resistances the patient also had to contend with the resistance of the analyst who, it sounds from your argument, would also have to change.

BION: I think so, certainly. I have given the example before of people who thought that projective algebraic geometry was incompatible with Euclidean geometry. There are certain respects in which these are different, but algebraic projective geometry is *implicit* in Euclidean geometry. Now, thanks to Descartes, what was implicit in Euclidean geometry has been made *explicit*. The same thing applies in this mutual situation: I usually have to point out to patients that they cannot come to me for analysis without—

whether they like it or not—having to analyse me. They may not like that because they don't know what sort of rage I might get into if they hit on the right thing; it is difficult to believe that the analyst would not take it badly in the way a child is quite used to: "I can't understand why you are *so* naughty"; it is made clear that when you are playing with your little brother or sister you shouldn't bash him or her on the head, you shouldn't bash each other; you ought to be playing nicely together. And so ought the analyst and the analysand. But, in fact, it is a pretty rough game.

Q: Could you differentiate between these kinds of processes of change and their consequences, from simply becoming maladjusted, losing friends and alienating people?

BION: No, I don't think that is at all easy, because it again involves this matter of direction. Mathematicians tried to deal with this by the introduction of vectors. Analytically we haven't discovered a way of dealing with it, so we don't know the direction. People choose to say that the world is in an awful mess today. Next step: it is due to this horrible psychoanalysis, all this damned nonsense about people's minds and personalities—*that* is what causes the trouble. It is very difficult to refute. But it would be useful if one could get any sort of clue as to how to assess direction, or in what way to presuppose a mental state in which one was travelling in some direction. The astronomers have decided that the solar system lies on one of the edges of the spiral nebula. The fact that there is no bright spot available at the centre is apparently regarded as what you would expect, because you can't see through the debris of the nebula itself to its centre. But it is supposed that beyond that, at a distance of 10^8 million light-years, lies the other side of the centre of ourselves. The scale of ephemeral creatures like ourselves is very hard to determine, very hard to see what direction is being taken by us. Indeed, with recent developments one could say that the human race itself is at the end of the road at a point where it is displaced by some other form of life. It is hardly a practical problem when we are dealing with these things on a relatively microscopic scale, not macroscopic—the macroscopic scales are not much use to us, but could throw some light on what is going on and on our being able to keep on the right track, assuming that there is a proper path for us to follow. Races which have a long history—such as the Jews, the Chinese—retain a certain cohesion so that they can get some idea about direction. But unfortunately these ancient cultures have also lost touch with their sources, their origins—or, as Freud put it, he doubted that Moses would understand his, Freud's, Hebrew.

It is a question of importance when one talks, as I do, about the truth. The answer seems to be so easily made, as Francis Bacon does in his essay: "'What is truth?' said jesting Pilate; and would not stay for an answer" [*Essays*, I, "Of Truth"]. We have to rely on our feelings; somehow at a certain point we feel, "Yes, that's right." Whether it is right or what the scale of reference is, or what the relationships to the truth are to the rest of truth, I don't know—and I don't know of any way in which we can get a grip on it. What we do know is that we are part and parcel of these vogues and can, to that extent, make some allowance for the pressure we experience.

Q: To what extent, in order to think the thoughts we think, do we require other thinkers at well?

BION: It may fall to a particular individual to be able to formulate the thought or idea. But I don't think the actual germination of the idea can be attributed to any particular individual. It is very difficult to locate that. It crops up in practice chiefly with people who think that they own ideas and are very sensitive to plagiarism. There seems to be something in it—one would like to claim a certain ownership of an idea, but whether that is anything other than the ordinary predatory instincts, I don't know. It could be part of the wish to grab, to carve out a sphere in the latest series of discoveries.

Q: I am wondering how much of what you have been saying approximates to the Jungian concept of the analyst as the agent or container.

BION: The relationship of one idea to another is quite a difficult problem because ideas are not so clearly defined as words—and that is bad enough. For purposes of verbal communication you can do a lot with dictionary definitions and the rules of grammar, but when it comes to ideas themselves—the real thing, whatever that is—I think it is extremely optimistic to imagine that they also conform to the ways in which we think or even express our thoughts or ideas. It seems to me that this is one of the places where the formulist mathematician gets into trouble. The assumption is that the logical capacity of the human mind is of very great importance—and so it is to us for purposes of thinking—but the Intuitionists represent a revolt (Brower, Heyting and others) against that particularly rigid structure that doesn't really leave room for growth. The problem is that the work of the Intuitionists is so difficult for most of us to understand at all. Contrast this with geometria. I mean by that what is to us now a rather magical use of numbers. For example, you take the letters of which your name is composed; they are placed in the alphabet, and you add them up and get a certain number. You can play that game more or less indefinitely. It isn't geometry: it's a sort of—religious mathematics? I don't know, but certainly a mathematics that is employed and does come to the surface in developments where there is a theological turmoil, one of these spaces in the total area of human thought where an upheaval begins to surface. I am thinking of it in terms of the total area of thought, sometimes called mathematical, sometimes religious, sometimes biochemical and so forth. These areas of turmoil, of emotional upheaval, break out spasmodically over the total sphere. There you get thrown up characteristics that seem to conform to those in other emotional outbursts. For example, one of the manifestations of vogue seems to be the messianic turmoil. This is peculiar because the messiah often disavows it but it is very strongly advocated by a sort of prophet. The actual centre of that particular turmoil—the messiah—is strongly affected by something outside the centre; it is ex-centric, like a situation where psychoanalysis itself becomes the vogue, and after a bit shifts onto somebody or something else—the latest vogue.

Q: Would you in this way be talking about psychoanalysis as the prophet of something that is much more central?

BION: I think there is something much more central—possibly of a kind formulated by Schopenhauer, who doesn't say much about it but simply describes it as "the energy to exist". It can surface in this way in Freud and in psychoanalysis as one of these temporary bubbles on the total surface. As usual in these turmoils—like the period of adolescence in the individual—various features that have been latent or unobserved beforehand become apparent, sometimes negatively; for the time being the turmoil is noticeable by being suppressed, by not being allowed to emerge. I think that with Freud, Stekel and Jung there was an attempt to apportion out the areas that would be occupied by those three particular forces, but I can't say that I find the struggle for possession of some particular sphere at all enthralling or important.

Q: Yesterday you made an analogy with a blind person using a stick to find his way about. Could you describe the instruments you use?

BION: No, I don't think so, certainly not anything I have been able to formulate. Somebody else might have a better idea of what I do use, particularly those who come to me for analysis. I am able to draw attention to the fact that coming to me for analysis is a vastly more unpleasant matter than coming to me for a supervision; it is a great shock to discover that. The actual close contact with an actual "me" is quite different from what they would suppose if they heard me talk. I can only suggest that anything I say about how I do it is probably somewhat misleading and off the beam. It has a lot to do with what I was trying to describe when I said, "When you are asleep you are in a different state of mind from the state of mind when you are awake." I am still talking about that when I refer to the patient who seems to behave physically in a way that could be seen as cataleptic. And the same thing applies to his state of mind: it is not dreaming and it is not wide awake. I don't know what it is, but it is very precarious and does seem to depend on being able to be on the edge of a precipice—to use a pictorial image. I think it can be seen with most patients, especially in a prolonged analysis; you can get to a point where it is much clearer that they also behave in such a way that they are aware—particularly in adolescence—that they are frightened of going mad. Later it becomes much more a case of being frightened of being *called* mad; I like to flatter myself now that I am sufficiently used to being called that not to mind it as much. But I am not so sure that I would if I were in Soviet Russia, for example, or subjected to certain other cultural forces. It amazes me sometimes that analysts really seem to believe that they will be permitted to be psychoanalysts—I don't know why. I'm not sure that we all ought not to be prepared to "go underground", as they say. Milton makes great play of the image of Alpheus, the river that disappears and emerges from time to time in different places. [See also seminars two and three.]

MATTI HARRIS: Perhaps we ought to stop now and all hope that Doctor Bion—who will, as far as we are concerned, have gone underground for the next year—will re-surface here next year at the same time and give us a comparable but different experience. I would like, on behalf of everybody, to give heartfelt thanks for the interesting time we have had. We have no doubt it has changed us in some way or another—we know not how.

BION: Thank you. I hope not to be put under arrest when I return to California on the grounds of having changed so much.

27 March 1979

[The "winter of discontent" began with a wave of industrial action at the end of 1978; by early 1979 Britain was paralysed by strikes, and the normal life of the country came perilously close to a complete halt.]

BION: *[first part of recording missing]* . . . an establishment, shall we say, like the government of this country; then it buds off plenty more, called "devolution", and each bit of the devolved thing takes in a whole lot of other people—so you get bigger and bigger bureaucracies. In this respect I think we in psychoanalysis are well in the mainstream: there's the British Psychoanalytic Society, there's the International Psychoanalytic Society, there's the European Psychoanalytic Society, and I don't know what else—there are plenty of them, all of them presumably with their distinguished people, all of them with the distinguished people swallowed up in the administration, never having a chance of getting near a patient because they have to spend so much time organizing things. This raises a very difficult problem—that of whether people who are engaged in thinking can indeed combine it in any way, and, if so, how?

Q: I am wondering if the individual's thinking in his own time is different from that of the group's time.

Bion: What happens to your feelings, opinions, ideas and theories when, as here, we all come together? They would appear to be sunk without a trace, swallowed up in the group where we would hope to get some kind of discussion or clarification of the problems with which we have to deal. But the curious thing is that as soon as we are contained in a group, it seems to be very difficult indeed to go in the direction of developing thoughts or ideas or feelings of our own; we are dominated by a need to be like everybody else and to think what everybody else thinks and feels—although how to tell what everybody else thinks or feels may be something we would find very difficult to formulate.

Somebody posed a question to me the other day—I can't say that I have found an answer to it, but I can pass it on. A small boy came for assistance, for help of some sort. As far as I could make out from the account I was given of this experience, on the one hand there was the analyst, and on the other this small boy who started drawing pictures with coloured chalks. The analyst gave an interpretation to which there was apparently no particular response; the small boy proceeded to draw another picture. And so it went on. He drew a picture of a lot of children on skateboards, but since I can't draw as well as he did, I do this [draws a few lines on the blackboard]. If I allow myself to get rather excited about it, I try to do another one [draws a few more lines]. Those are two signs, parts of my conversation with you. If you ask me what that sounds like, you probably couldn't hear I was producing my version of the Blue Danube Waltz. You couldn't hear it and I can't make the noise sufficiently clear here, not even with the apparatus of loudspeakers and so forth. I doubt very much whether you would recognize much more than a faint hiss. So one could say: that is the language, that is the pictograph, and the pronunciation of it is that funny noise I was making; that is how you say it if you want to talk it instead of drawing it. But suppose someone scientific came along: "Do you mean to say that that was a Viennese waltz, that row you were making? The Blue Danube? Have you ever seen the Danube? It's a dirty, muddy stream that moves at a tremendous pace. What are you talking about?" So there is this problem of the scientific view, the "true view", and then these various other views like my drawing of someone on a skateboard that certainly is not an accurate view. What is the nature of the communication? Which are you going to take? You can start making signs, like A, B, C—the alphabetic script—or you can start making pictographs, the sort of thing the Chinese do.

Freud called an international psychoanalytic meeting hoping it would be the start of an international communication between people. In fact, instead of it ending as he had hoped, it ended in all sorts of disagreements. Typical of that was the disagreement between Jung and Freud as to what was psychoanalysis and who was entitled to use the term. So there is this problem—as for example here—of how we can see any particular way in which we can communicate with each other. Is there any common language that we can talk so that we can have a discussion?

Q: There is, apparently, a shared assumption about something called "the Establishment" that is "other people": they are powerful, they are boring and, above all, one must not be like that. If one actually looks at the people who reach a position of importance, it isn't very accurate.

BION: No. The only accurate thing about it is probably the feeling of the individual who talks like that, but not necessarily, because individuals do not have to speak the truth about what they think or feel. But I think it is a fair assumption to suppose that the individual does try to communicate accurately—at any rate, in this sort of community. When it comes to groups of people at war, that is different; then they do not necessarily want to communicate what they think or what their plans are.

Are we somewhat prematurely and precociously attempting to achieve a kind of cooperative endeavour when in fact we are not really capable of doing much more than wage war against each other? Is it a matter of domination of who is top, who did it first, who is the owner, who possesses it? It depends on what sort of culture, what sort of civilization we live in.

To revert to the dominating silence, the thing that reduces us all to silence because we are frightened of expressing our true opinion or saying what we really mean—or, for that matter, meaning what we really say: if the Establishment, or the dominating force, is one that is exerted in the direction of making everybody conform to a particular attitude or outlook, then it matters very much what the nature of that culture or group is and how individual members—people who would like to be able to respect themselves and even, if possible, respect other people—are to compete with this pressure to be uniform, all to think alike, all to be equal. Péguy [1873–1914], quoting *"liberté, egalité, fraternité"*, said [in *Basic Verities*] that two of those are completely different from the third; two of those aspirations are really worthy of pursuit, but not so the third [*egalité*]. I don't know if that gives any idea as to what bunch of thoughts, ideas or feelings would come nearer to expressing our present culture: liberty? equality? fraternity? That is simplifying the problem by tacking it onto those three terms.

Q: I feel that pauses and silences in a group play an important role in understanding—just as they do in music.

Bion: That is true, and in psychoanalysis also. Long ago I was asked, "Do you only just talk?" I said, "No, we don't; sometimes we are silent." Of course, that also has something to do with the beginning of the sound because the silence contributes a meaning to the sounds, to the rhythm. Even in silence we are giving a great deal of primacy to the verbal communication. I think it is reasonable because although it is a recent achievement, this ability to communicate by means of articulate speech—by recent I mean only a few hundred thousand years—seems to have been so productive that it can be looked to as a possible way of approaching the kind of problems with which we are concerned. That doesn't mean to say that it is an adequate method of communication. Hence one cannot very well say—though it is quite easy to do so—that because the small boy insists on saying nothing but just goes on drawing, he is resisting. Resisting what? He is merely disagreeing that the method of communication is verbal. He doesn't stop the analyst from making a verbal communication—he just goes on making a pictorial point of view, a pictorial communication. When it comes

---

[I think it worth while quoting at some length from Charles Péguy's *Basic Verities*, which greatly impressed Bion: see Appendix A.]

to huge bunches of people—like the Chinese—there it becomes a very serious matter if we think, "Oh, these Chinese, you know, this pictorial stuff, they don't even know how to write from left to right. These Orientals have nothing to contribute to our civilization." But when we have small groups like this, is there any chance of getting any further with this problem? Or are we all still dominated by the need to be "top", or to join the group that is "top", or to join the group or person who has the biggest number of possessions? Now we might almost say, "the biggest number of mental possessions"—that is to say, the area in which it is supposed that there are such things as creations of the mind. According to Plato, Socrates said he was merely a midwife, he merely helped people to give birth to their ideas. How much progress do you think we have made in the art of mental obstetrics? To what extent are we capable of tolerating anybody who could make a contribution? Or are we wiser to remain silent, to refrain from our own particular method of communication? I am not saying that the only method of communication is verbal—that, unfortunately, is about all I am capable of—but there are plenty of people who are not so limited, who are capable of musical composition, of painting, or even of verbal communication of a very high order. But is this the sort of culture that promotes or makes possible the creative efforts of those who are able to create? Here we are supposed to be able to express our opinion on this matter.

Q: With reference to the child who went on drawing while the analyst was talking, I am wondering if that is real communication if it is not taken in by anyone else.

BION: This is the problem. Supposing you have something to say: you unfortunately have to have somebody who is prepared to listen. If you are capable of painting, there has to be someone who will look at the thing—and as you know, most people don't. Most people will drift through famous galleries without a clue to what is in them. As an example, a person goes to the National Gallery and says, "I could have got through in half the time if I had . . . boots." That is one way of looking at the National Gallery—you don't have to bother about the paintings, especially as, if you allowed yourself to look at them, it would take up a very great deal of time. Of course, my example is ridiculous, but it isn't a ridiculous problem; in fact we don't have a great deal of time, and it is very difficult indeed to know how to apportion such time as we think we have available. That is one reason why, as an analyst, I would like to be able to express myself clearly so that the patient doesn't have to waste too much time trying to make out what on earth I am talking about. So in this curious way the exactitude of expression is likely to become a very demanding component, whether you are a painter or a musician or a speaker, so that you express yourself as economically as possible in the hope that someone will bother to listen to you and will be able to listen as economically as possible.

Q: As regards communication, the problem with art is to decide when it is not art. This question was raised in a recent controversy over a painting in the Tate Gallery.

BION: I think you are right. It raises the whole question of discrimination because it is so important to be able to distinguish between the fake and the real thing. There are plenty of painters who are extremely capable of giving a very good representation of, say, trees in a forest or a wood. But there is a great deal of difference between that and a painting of trees by Cézanne. I wouldn't like to say what the difference is, especially when we have all been taught to believe that Cézanne was a great painter—so we don't have to bother about that any more. But if we do bother about it, then we might tell the difference between a painting by Cézanne and a very technically able reproduction of it. That depends on this capacity for discrimination and the fact that it is very difficult to exercise it.

The attempt to use articulate speech for the expression of problems was by no means what articulate speech was elaborated for; its roots, the savage methods of behaviour, had to become civilized. We are still in the position of being savage animals who have to tame each other. But when violence is opposed to discussion, it does seem as if the outcome is doubtful, because the person who wants to discuss may have to defend himself, or the nation that wants to discuss may have to defend itself or even the right to speak. For example, psychoanalysis or communities of people who are wedded to discussion might become very unwelcome to the

authorities. It could be regarded as subversive and an encourage-
ment to people to have ideas of their own. You only have to look
back through history to see the attempts that were made to sup-
press philosophical discussion or religious discussion, or any other
form of discussion. But there is usually some little escape, like a
seed pod, carried by the wind, that sprouts up somewhere else.

Galen [Claudius Galenus, c.130 A.D.–c.200 A.D.], a revolutionary
thinker who really believed in observation of the human body,
finally became a sort of god whose opinion was never to be questioned; free thought was suppressed, and anatomy and physiology
stood still for generations—until it sprouted up in artists like
Leonardo and Raphael who decided to look at the human body, the
cadaver, and draw pictures of it. Then, through that kind of lateral
expression, it came back to anatomy; anatomists again started
looking at the human body. It is commonplace that students have
to draw pictures of their detections; anybody who has been a
medical student knows how much we disliked having to dissect
and to draw accurate pictures of what we saw. Sounds simple,
doesn't it? All you have to do is to draw what you see—don't tell
lies about it, don't invent fabulous systems of circulation and so
forth, but draw what you see. But it is not at all infrequent for
medical students never to recover from their experience of the
dissecting-room. Do you think it is going to be any better with the
dissection of the human mind, character or personality?

There would be something very queer about any analytic experience—whether one identifies with the analyst or the analysand—
in which it didn't become clear that both parties dislike that
occupation. It is not possible to analyse the analysand without
being analysed oneself by the patient. So both parties are almost
inevitably engaged in an occupation that arouses feelings of hatred
and anger—not to mention also the wish to run away, to fly from
that occupation. That is one reason why the future of psychoanalysis is always very precarious. Suppose it was suppressed and then
leaked out again in, say, the direction of painters who depicted the
character or the soul of the sitter. Only the other day I heard about
Graham Sutherland's protest at the destruction of his painting of
Winston Churchill. I dare say it would have been much better if he
had stuck to photography because you can get away with it on the

grounds that it is only what the camera shows. But a brilliant painter may depict the character, and this can excite a great deal of hostility on the part of the beholder. It isn't simply a question of finding somebody to listen to what you say; you also have to find somebody who will look at the painting that you paint. The little boy had to find somebody who would look at his drawings of people on skateboards. What is the analyst to do about it? If he sticks to making verbal interpretations, it can easily sound as if it is an attempt to maintain the superiority of verbal as opposed to artistic communication. Plenty of people have been written off as stupid or foolish simply because their methods of communication are different from what we ourselves are used to, or different from what we are able to understand.

Q: Coming full circle, I think analysts had better understand groups and institutions if they are going to understand their patients and the task they are dealing with, as well as dealing with the internal world.

BION: In much the same way it matters if the diameter of the circle becomes so great that it may not appear to be the diameter at all because the segment of the circle seems to be very like a straight line. In other words, the debate can become so wide that there is virtually no communication. Suppose all this kind of debate took place 10^8 million light-years ago: we have no method of communication with the past, and indeed it is difficult now to say what we owe to our forebears, who stopped using grunts and expressions of rage and fear and tried to communicate either by visible signs or some other method. I don't think that can be explained simply by Mendelian inheritance because, as I understand it, that communication would depend upon the inheritance of acquired characteristics. In other words, if we could start where our parents left off, and if we could leave off at a point at which our children could take over, then we might get an inheritance of acquired characteristics, we could become wiser people. Even aspirations like United Nations, United States, United Kingdom might begin to become realized; there might be such a thing as United People. There might even be an agreement about the need to promote the kind of activities pursued by philosophers, painters, musicians, poets, as part of a united effort, not so much as to who, which tiny scrap, has won the championship, as it were, but as part of the general mood. It took a very long time before we became as civilized as we are, and it may take a very long time still before we become more or adequately civilized. By "civilized", I don't mean like everybody else; I mean a situation where we could have respect for ourselves and other selves, while at the same time remaining part of the community.

Q: As I said before, analysts had better understand more about their own institutions . . .

BION: I certainly think that if we can, we should devote such capacity as we have to things that are within our reach—in the sense of being near enough to be observable and comprehensible—so that we could at least make some contribution towards comprehending them.

In the experience of analysis it is curious how often we find that the analysand is most unwilling to admit the importance of any particular excellence that he has. Patients don't really mind devoting their attention to their crimes, their faults, their mistakes, and very often would like to get the analyst to agree to become a sort of "father confessor" to dole out appropriate penances. But when it comes to something the patient can do really well, it is extraordinary how often that same patient will denigrate it, dislike it and not want to pursue it any further, on the grounds that it is too easy or that it comes "naturally", as if doing something that is natural is a sort of crime itself. There are many things that are natural to us—such as fighting each other—and it may be true that we need to be discriminating and decide what is desirable and what undesirable. Whether we can do so with any degree of accuracy is another matter; we simply have to make a decision in the light of our own prejudices. I have a prejudice: I remember a time when I was extremely anxious to join the army and get mixed up with the glorious occupation of war, but having tried shooting people—and getting shot at—I don't like it. I think there is still a good deal to be said for standing up for one's ideas.

Q: The army must be a group in which it is difficult to know what one's own ideas are.

BION: Yes. I have known a person undergo the whole of army discipline and then give up the military career to become an actor. So it does happen that we join a particular profession and then chuck it up, but it is rare. Most of us may feel we have made a mistaken choice, but the upheaval involved in changing it, rectifying our mistake, is too painful; we would prefer to go on with the same profession, same theories, same ideas and not change them.

Q: Do you think it is really an addiction to go on with what we don't really like?

BION: The only thing is to question oneself as to whether one is addicted or not. For example, I choose to be a psychoanalyst, but I wouldn't be able to say with any certainty whether that is simply an addiction—in the rather pejorative sense. I would like to be able to say that I am devoted to the occupation of analysis, or to helping my fellow men. But it is very difficult to know if one is devoted to a worthy object or has become addicted to that object. It is an ongoing problem from which we shall never be free.

Q: Could you say something about the difference between "devoted to" and "addicted to"?

BION: Take an example like being devoted to one's family welfare. While everybody may agree that the patient is devoted, when looked at more closely that same person doesn't give a damn what happens to the family as long as it contributes to the glory of the parent, so long as the child does credit to its father or mother. I would call that not devotion to the family, but an addiction. I would want to introduce some sort of pejorative term into my own private formulation of that particular character.

Q: Would you say that it is a form of addiction if a person cares only about his or her own family, while the rest of the world can go hang?

BION: One would have to have some idea about the motive of that person. It might be apparently extremely patriotic to want the welfare of one's own nation. But it is also true that if one's nation were well off, we would share in the general prosperity. There we are up against a profound problem—as we are in this subject all the time. It starts off as something simple, blossoms out straight away, and we then find that we are dealing with profound matters.

Is there anything particularly harmful in being a member of a nation that is well off and in sharing in the general prosperity? It doesn't do anyone any harm apparently. Eric Gill said that the best thing he could hope for the English nation was that it would become poor and impoverished. I don't know if he would have liked getting mixed up with the sort of traffic jams that I have experienced here—I would rather get here easily and comfortably without any fuss. So that particular statement of a general principle may be impeccable in terms of logic, but one does want the person who is stating it to practise what he preaches, and also to preach what is practicable. But the only person one has any control over is likely to be oneself. So we can try to live up to our principles—or to have principles it is possible to live up to.

Q: I have been thinking about the way we use time as a container.

BION: Do we use time? Or does time use us? This is one of these extremely useful terms: most of us use it in a limited sort of way; we can look at a watch or a clock and schedule our day according to the number of hours we think are available. But when it comes to closer and more scientific investigation of what we mean by "time", it becomes clear that it is no good just looking it up in the dictionary. What do we mean by "time"? The point has often been stressed: "Time, like an ever-rolling stream, bears all its sons away; they fly forgotten, as a dream dies at the opening day" [Isaac Watts (1674–1748), Psalms, 90]. There certainly seems to be some force with every one of us that contributes to the fact of one's birth and one's decline. We cannot really say it is due to time, but it is closely associated with the passage of time—as we understand it. The question should be much more, "What do you mean by 'using time', or by 'being contained in it'?"

Q: I had a patient who seemed to travel backwards in time. His material was all about the past and at times had been so repetitive that I might have one whole year of sessions of the same material, the same words. I really thought I would die with impatience and boredom. Instead of moving on in the river of time, he appeared to me to be on the bank, as if he hated time. I am thinking about the problem of tolerating someone who seems to hate time as much as that.

BION: It certainly sounds like a peculiar kind of omnipotence if a patient feels that he can act a superior plot to all the rest of the flotsam and jetsam going down the stream, as if saying, "Yes, all these people go down the stream, but I—I'm saved; I've clambered out onto the shore." One wonders what sort of standards are being used there.

Q: It is comfortable.

BION: Yes. You don't always have to take analgesics or hypnotics to be comfortable; you can achieve it with ideas. And indeed, it *is* comfortable to feel that we have now achieved a certain system of thoughts and ideas, and very *un*comfortable to feel that the whole lot of them might be upset by somebody who questions them—for example, by talking in a community like this. One can try to use one's theories as a sort of impenetrable armour plate.

Q: Do we have to tolerate social upheaval if there is to be growth?

BION: I think it is fairly easy to say that there has to be space for growth or development if we stick to geographical measures, say of land, air, food, and so on. But the same thing applies to the domain of the mind, Falling back on metaphorical language, there has to be space available for mental growth. This habit we all have of wrapping our ideas around ourselves to keep out the cold so that we will never have another thought, never be upset by somebody else's thoughts, may be very comfortable, but it does not allow space for the development of ideas. And if the unfortunate person who does that then grows, this comfortable state of mind begins to be restrictive, the suit of mental clothes becomes too tight—that is the misfortune in being the victim of these growth processes. Whether we like it or not, there is always the danger that we might have ideas or thoughts of our own, and those thoughts and ideas may want us to express them, want to be given a chance, an opportunity for expression. To fall back on the Socratic idea, there might be thoughts that want to be born, want to be aided out into a situation where they could grow and express themselves. So, from that point of view, every person has to be a midwife to his own ideas, thoughts and feelings.

The idea of being comfortable is very seductive—you only have to go outside to see the advertisements that are bombarding us on all sides to draw attention to how well off we would be *if* we had so-and-so's patent nostrum. There are plenty of invitations to be comfortable, but it is a problem to know how to discriminate between the fake and the real thing.

28 March 1979

Q : I am wondering if there is a psychoanalytic way to the truth.

BION: None whatever. Psychoanalysis is only a technical instrument, something we can make use of for any purpose we want—to make confusion worse confounded, or to mislead or deceive people, and so on. It all depends on who is making use of it. Is this building for the use of psychoanalysis, or have psychoanalysts been made use of in order to build this building? Are the available rooms conducive to the pursuit of psychoanalytic efforts? Or are they not?

The profound question in that is the problem of whether the person who purports to be searching for the truth is genuinely trying to arrive at the truth, or is a fake, an artificial representation of a seeker after truth. It is a very difficult question to answer. If you felt you could rely on your own judgment about that, then you might be able to tell whether somebody's paintings or writings are the work of a real genius. But as for the technical accomplishments of psychoanalysis, that doesn't tie you down at all—you can do what you like. Any idea that it inevitably causes you to speak the truth or discover the truth is pure rubbish.

Q: Yesterday you were speaking about patients' reluctance to talk about their own achievements. I am wondering why that is so difficult to do. Is it something linked with the harsh superego that prevents emotional enjoyment and development?

BION: From time to time one can find various characteristics that seem to be related to obstruction. For example, this point where we can detect from a person's behaviour and discussion that there is a moral system emerging from it. We could say that the patient appears to be dominated by very powerful moral impulses. If we had the opportunity to go on listening to and observing the patient, then it might become possible to draw his attention to the very important part that his morals were playing in the analytic experience. Perhaps we could go on further and get a bit clearer what kind of moral system this is. Psychoanalytically, theoretically and in certain religious approaches, it is also believed that there are very powerful feelings of guilt—original sin. But that sort of impulse seems to develop into a peculiar kind of moral system in which we can detect certain characteristics that do occur—namely, the moral system that seems to tell us what is wrong but never gives any inkling of what is right, that can be so dominant in the patient's mind that he doesn't dare to be or do anything. I say, "in the patient's mind", but it doesn't necessarily have to be so; I think it can also be in the society, an institution like this one, or the institution of psychoanalysis, or the Houses of Parliament—anything that can be dominated by this negative, prohibitive attitude. It is clearly described in the Book of Genesis and again in the story of the Tower of Babel, the idea being to find out what these creatures are up to, tell them not to, and stop it. That seems to some of us to be a very negative attitude, the kind of thing that is rather unimportant, in the way that a child doesn't know enough about running its own life or anybody else's to fill adequately the position of dominating the family. But one hopes that parents, who have more experience of life, may be prohibitory; they may often be reduced to saying, "Don't do this", or "Don't do that", but that is much milder than the kind of moral system to which I am referring.

At some point we have to be critical of our moral outlook and ask ourselves to what extent it is, in fact, being prohibitive.

Q: Could you comment on the relationship between the internal process, and what sort of external requirements are needed to set the process going, and perhaps keep it in being.

BION: In practice I find that it is important to be able to draw the patient's attention to just your question: it is surprising how difficult that is. The patient can express quite a lot of opinions and views, and it becomes clearer that he is dominated by some particular train of thought. But why today? What is going on? What has triggered this off? I don't know what words to use; I don't know how to draw the patient's attention to the problem—namely, what has started him off on it.

Take one example: a patient expresses some degree of emotion, and the analyst says, "I think you are being affected by the fact that this is the week-end break when I do not usually see you", or it could be any other break in the analysis. If that is correct, it could be the trigger for that particular session's dominating theme. But in fact, it is very difficult to know.

A session may seem to be extremely disjointed: I have sometimes then been able to draw the patient's attention to the fact that he was just going to tell me something and was then interrupted. That interruption may be from outside—some noise or something I have done. But when that goes on happening, when I find that the patient cannot apparently pursue a train of thought at all, I wonder whether I am missing the train of thought he *is* expressing, or whether in fact he is constantly interrupted, constantly thrown off the road on which he is wanting to travel, the theme of his discourse, the theme he is wanting to talk to me about.

I'll try to imitate it: "Well, I was coming to the clinic just now— you know what I mean—there was a fellow on a bicycle, and he suddenly emerged from the side of the road and, er, well, er, that reminds me—the other day when I was going to talk to my son— now I've forgotten what I was going to say—er—let me think. Oh yes, I remember, yes, I think that this school to which he is going is very bad. They are always . . ." and so on. We have all encountered people who talk in that kind of way. You end up wondering whether you are talking to somebody who has something wrong with his mental apparatus, or whether he is in fact being interrupted and, if so, why? It can be that a person is very sensitive, has excellent hearing and is interrupted by noises from outside, but sometimes it is not so. Where, then, is the source of that interruption? You may not be able to answer that, but if you don't, this kind of patient still goes on pouring out more and more for ten minutes, a quarter of an hour, half an hour of disjointed sentences—it is impossible to see any theme running through it. Sometimes the interruption seems to be more permanent—not a series of interruptions but an obstruction amounting to a permanent blockage of the patient's train of thought—and then he has to find some sort of permanent circulatory diversion. If we were talking about the body, we could say that the patient has an embolus; the arterial system has been interrupted and then there has to be set up a collateral circulation.

Such a blockage can occur in a very gifted child who may never get back again to its main capacity for expressing itself, whether artistic, scientific or whatever. But we hope that, with the analytic discussion, it may be possible to draw attention to that blockage, including this peculiar kind of moral blockage. We are not disapproving of a moral system, but suggesting that it could be a matter for discussion as to what this system is that makes it virtually impossible for the analyst to be right, for the patient to be right, for his family to be right, and so on in his various relationships. If we can do that, then we make it less necessary for the patient to resort to that kind of collateral circulation.

Q: Could you give me your opinion on the nature of envy as a
    component of a moral system?

BION: No, I can't, because I think it is worth considering as being almost a fundamental, very powerful characteristic. You can see it where the patient—one hopes it is the patient and not the analyst— is so envious both of his analyst and of himself for making good use of the analyst that he cannot tolerate anything in the nature of successful or profitable analysis, even when he himself is one of the rewarded participants.

We unfortunately have to use these terms; it is one of the ways in which splitting has been turned to good account. We split things up—envy, hate, admiration and so forth—to make articulate speech more or less possible. But, of course, we don't in fact split up anything—these grammatical divisions and rules of articulate speech are quite all right for the purposes of articulate speech but not at all suitable for describing the human mind. I find it somewhat easier to think of envy and gratitude as being on the same linear progression; they are not really separable, but one is the extreme of the other, as if they were polarized, as if these sorts of feelings could be spoken of as polarized activities. [See Melanie Klein's "Envy and Gratitude".]

Q: I was thinking that in the first three years you came here the weather was very warm; my expectation somehow was that this time it would be the same . . .

BION: . . . as long as you don't hold me responsible for having done it on purpose! There must be an explanation for this kind of weather; the meteorologists make an attempt at a scientific description of it. We can see on TV approaching low pressure just off the island there, and something else just off the island there, and between the two of them there are probably going to be fine intervals and a good deal of sleet and snow, and so on—most uncomfortable. It is an attempt to get to the truth of what it is that really affects the weather. But the truth is independent of us. Psychoanalysis is an attempt to know what it is that interrupts us, or makes it impossible to think clearly or to have any respect for the facts that are available to us; it is an attempt to investigate what it is in ourselves that causes so much trouble, not because we cause the trouble but because it is the only thing about which we can say anything at all. We can do nothing about these powers and forces that are out of our control. So if we are ourselves at fault, then it is useful to know what is the matter. "The fault, dear Brutus, is not in our stars, but in ourselves, that we are underlings" [Shakespeare, *Julius Caesar*, I.ii]—a most profound statement. Sooner or later there will have to be a method by which the faults in ourselves have to be corrected by ourselves. This is familiar to us when it comes to clinical matters: when we have a physical complaint we have to get some sort of help—an ambulance, a doctor or a nurse; that is commonplace. But it is a much more difficult problem with regard to defects in our method of thinking. There has to be created what we call a psychoanalyst, or something better—the name is not of much importance, but it *is* of importance that the "thing itself" should exist. There should be people to whom we could look for some sort of assistance about these "blockages", this fact that we are not necessarily stupid but that we don't seem to be able to think clearly. Actors can be afraid of "blackouts" or stage fright; it is the fear of these "interruptions" that interferes with their ability to exercise their technical capacity.

Q: With reference to your comments about the man running round the National Gallery and not understanding that there was something good on the walls, how can we make something available to someone who lacks this understanding?

BION: I don't see any way in which we can evade that difficulty. We can know about its existence and be warned, have some foresight about it. But in the practice of analysis it ceases to be a matter of theoretical, high-powered discussion; it becomes a matter of detecting it in the actual psychoanalytic episode when two people meet together with that kind of object. It is truly dreadful the way in which psychoanalytic theory can become so learned, so prestigious, that I would certainly hate to try to understand it myself; in fact, I don't waste my time trying to. I do occasionally get bombarded with it: while trying to say something to me, the patient is constantly interrupted by his own high-powered psychoanalytic knowledge. There is the same difficulty at the other pole, where there appears to be an inability to understand or to appreciate the reality of analysis. It is a curious fact that even in physical medicine doctors or surgeons can become callous; having to deal constantly with physical pain, they become almost insensitive to it. There are occasions when it erupts: I had the experience of a surgeon and an anaesthetist having such a nice time that they failed to observe that the child on the operating table had very nearly died. They suddenly ceased enjoying the joke and started putting emergency measures into action—unfortunately too late. [See *All My Sins Remembered*, p. 40.]

We can become callous to the actual nature of the pain, whether it is physical or mental. I know from my own experience that one loses sight of the fact that the patient is suffering—and you are helped by the patient to lose sight of that. A patient may be so amusing that the session is quite enjoyable; it seems almost unkind to remember that that patient has come because he is suffering.

The numbers of things that make the cooperation between analyst and analysand very vulnerable are legion—there is no limit to them. We can only hope to be able to detect, in time, whatever is menacing that particular attempt at a creative cooperation between the two people. One comfort we have is that, in a way, analysis is not very important; it is a temporary affair and a temporary association. So we can talk about "transference" and "countertransference"; it is transferred, it is on the way, but the real point about it is that people are constantly having an uncomfortable relationship with each other—it may be with a group of people or with an individual person—and frequently the obstruction to the comfortable or pleasant relationship causes a collateral circulation to set up. If two people cannot succeed in the aspiration to become husband and wife, then they can fall back on the physical solution of it by turning it into a kind of successful sexual experience. I pick on that deliberately because we are so used to hearing that it is sexual inhibitions that cause trouble—and so they do. But sexual freedom also causes trouble; it is a method of finding a collateral circulation to avoid the difficulties of what one might call a spiritual relationship between two people—if that doesn't have too much of a moral connotation. But people can crave for a relationship that is additional to a purely sexual one; or they can crave for a physical relationship in addition to a purely intellectual discussion. I don't think these things are settled by simply feeling, "Oh, yes, sexual inhibitions." That is one possibility, but what we really need is to be able to detect where the blockage occurred and what form the collateral circulation has taken. I am sure that analysts who work with children must be familiar with the situation in which they feel that the real blockage is something between the husband and wife, and the collateral circulation is to send their child to an analyst. So the analyst + child is a kind of collateral circulation of something that lies outside that relationship. This is one of the complexities of our approach to these difficulties; that is why I say it is the old system of co-ordinates by which one can localize the pain. It is quite easy to flog away at the relationship between analyst and analysand, to go on analysing ad infinitum—as I said before, transference, countertransference and so forth—without really being able to locate where the real trouble lies.

Take this point about the weather: it isn't the only thing we notice on coming back to this country; there are also noticeable peculiarities of the state of mind. I don't know to what extent anything is done about that. For quite a long time I have thought it extraordinary that this is the only country to have fought two Great Wars from start to finish and not lost either of them. So it would hardly be surprising if we didn't now have to pay for that sort of luxury. Of course, I cannot pretend that that is a correct interpretation, or indeed that it is relevant; we do not know what are these changes in attitude, what the difference is between, shall we say, an England in which there is a belief in the British Empire, and an England nearer to conforming with what used to be called the attitude of Little Englanders. It is now little England, and the process of readjustment to these "facts" is very difficult. Anyway, we do not know what the facts are, nor what would be a readjustment on the right track. That seems to me to be one of the reasons why the work we do is urgent and needs to have a realistic slant to it. It is hopeless if bunches of people meet together and argue about Kleinian theory or somebody else's theory—it is a pure waste of time because there are far more important matters to think about, or even to learn to think about.

Extract from Péguy's *Basic Verities*

"Not only are the three terms of the republican device, Liberty, Equality, Fraternity not on the same plane, but the last two, which are nearer to each other than both are near the first, present several notable differences. Fraternity obliges us to tear our fellow men from destitution. That is a preliminary duty. Contrarily, equality is a far less pressing duty. Whereas it is intensely pressing and alarming to know that there are men still in want, the knowledge that, outside of destitution, men possess more or less large slices of riches does not worry me. I cannot profess much interest in the famous question of knowing to whom bottles of champagne, blooded horses, castles in the Loire valley, will belong in the city of the future. I hope that this will be settled somehow. But I really don't care if so and so has such and such a position, as long as there will really be a city from which no man can be banished or held in exile by economic destitution. Doubtless many other problems will engross the attention of citizens, but to nullify the civic pact it would be sufficient that a single man be wittingly held or, what comes to the same, be wittingly left in destitution. As long as one man remains outside, the door slammed in his face closes a city of injustice and hatred.

"The problem of destitution is not on the same plane, or of the same order as the problem of inequality. Here again, the old, traditional preoc-

Basic Verities, by Charles Péguy, was first published in England in 1943 by Kegan Paul, Trench, Tubner & Co. Ltd. (Prose and Poetry in French with English translation by Ann & Julian Green.)

cupations, instinctive to humanity, are found, when analysed, to be much deeper, far better justified, far more real than the recent and always artificial manifestations of democracy. To save the destitute is one of the oldest cares of noble humanity, persisting throughout all civilizations. From age to age, fraternity, whether it puts on the guise of charity or the guise of solidarity; whether it is practised towards a guest in the name of Zeus Hospitable; whether it welcomes the poor as an image of Jesus Christ or whether it establishes a minimum wage for workmen; whether it invests the citizen of the world, introducing him by baptism into the universal communion; or whether by the improvement of economic conditions it introduces him into the international city, this fraternity is a living, deep-rooted, imperishable human sentiment. . . .

"Compared with this great sentiment, the sentiment of equality will appear small. Also, less simple. When all men are provided with the necessities, the real necessities, with bread and books, what do we care about the distribution of luxury? Sentiments of fraternity must be formidable to have held in check, since the beginnings of humanity, all the sentiments of war, of barbarity, of hatred, and to have won over them. On the other hand, the sentiment of equality is not an old sentiment, a perpetual sentiment, a universal sentiment of first magnitude. At determined periods it appears in the history of humanity as a peculiar phenomenon, as a manifestation of the democratic spirit. In a certain sense, sentiments of fraternity have always animated great men and great peoples, animated them, disquieted them, for preoccupation about destitution never goes without bitterness, disquietude. The sentiment of equality, on the other hand, has never inspired anything but questionable, particular revolutions. It brought about that English revolution which bequeathed to the modern world such a nationalistic, imperialistic England. It brought about that American revolution which established such an imperialistic republic. It has not inaugurated humanity. It has not prepared the city. It has only inaugurated democratic governments. It is a composite, mixed, often impure sentiment to which vanity, envy and cupidity contribute. Fraternity disquiets, moves, passionately interests deep, serious-minded, hard-working, modest souls. Equality often reaches only men loving the limelight, men loving publicity, and men of government. Or again, sentiments of equality are artificial sentiments, sentiments obtained by formal construction; bookish, scholastic sentiments. When violent passions, deep and broad, human and popular are roused on behalf of equality, as happened at the beginning of the French Revolution, it is almost always because formal equality coincides with realities of liberty and fraternity. It is a fact that, save for rare exceptions, the men who introduced preoccupations of equality into politics were not, had not been, destitute. They were middle-class men and poor men, notaries, lawyers, attorneys, men who had not received the indelible investiture of destitution."

Interview by Anthony G. Banet, Jr.
Los Angeles, April 1976

BANET: In *Experiences in Groups*, you allude to your wartime experiences. I'd like to hear more about that.

BION: During the First World War, I went straight from school into the army and into the tanks because I wanted to see what a tank was. At that time they were still secret. I spent the rest of my time regretting it. It's very difficult to talk about the regret.

The military is a most peculiar business, because you are with a person only briefly, but you find that you get to know him quickly, very well, and in depth. There's nothing like this business of constantly being confronted with the probability of death. We had something like 700 officers come through our battalion in the short space of time in which we were in action—just about eighteen months. The result is that I knew individuals very, very well, but I would forget their names because I saw them so briefly. I remember coming across a fellow who wasn't in my company, but he recognized me. He was an AA scout—one of these people who go

This interview took place on 3 April and was published in *Group & Organization Studies*, Vol. 1, No. 3, September 1976.

about on motorcycles. I recognized his face when he introduced himself to me, but I could not place him. But that's the kind of thing that helped me to see that I really felt extremely deeply about the people I knew

BANET: It sounds like a very stressful time. Did these experiences contribute to your theoretical formulations about groups?

BION: No, not really, but I suppose they had some influence. It is such a hard thing to describe. In my first combat action, I had the intense feeling that I must not get frightened—I must not run away. (Of course, you can't run away—it's impossible—you discover that.) Another thing that you discover is that you don't settle anything in combat. You become more and more frightened, because you get to know more and more what the dangers are. That, I think, was a very unpleasant discovery. Mind you, I think that a good soldier, a regular soldier, can learn a very great deal. He doesn't become less frightened, but he knows how to look after himself.

BANET   The fear never leaves you.

BION: Never.

BANET: Were you practising medicine or psychiatry at that time?

BION: No, that came later. I was simply a combatant soldier. The curious thing was the great relief I felt when it was over, and then the discovery that, in fact, it had left very deep marks indeed.

I went straight up to Oxford after the war, and it was marvellous. Everything at the university was so exciting and so interesting, but it simply made it impossible to work out anything that had been simmering inside me. When I was at Oxford, there were a lot of tragedies of ex-service personnel. Another thing—the college authorities were surprised to find that virtually all officers were extremely well disciplined. There was no trouble whatsoever. A lot of people had expected a return of the "licentious soldier". We were seduced into a belief that everything was beautiful—as indeed it was. But it was very hard to realize why, while everything was so magnificent, we did not feel the privilege of enjoying it. Always, there was just a shadow of some kind—a frightful thing that never really left our minds. We simply attached it to new tasks like getting through finals, but I'm certain that the shadow of war was a background for all of us.

BANET: But the shadow was not talked about.

BION: Not talked about, no. Evelyn Waugh described it, rather to my surprise, I must say, when he said what a relief it was to get rid of our whole crowd, because we simply put a damper on the whole university. The university was overshadowed, from his point of view, by the ex-servicemen and the war people who were a dead weight. You couldn't make progress; you couldn't get through this "crust". Of course, he was sitting on top of the university. From our own point of view, we rather resented the "kids", so to speak, who had no war service and who thought they were the big noises of the university. But that didn't matter, of course, because we had so much more experience. I think that the university did suffer from having this great mass of ex-service people there.

There was the attempt to be very nice to the ex-servicemen, but the others didn't know what our problems were. All they could do was to give us comfortable rooms, good food and all of the creature comforts. From the point of view of the university authorities, there was very little that they could do about us. We were very pleased to plunge ourselves into all the diverse activities that existed. I was fortunate because I was a pretty good athlete. I was captain of the Oxford University Swimming Club. So I had plenty to occupy myself. I also played rugby for the university. I'm not sure whether it was really lucky or not, because it enabled us to cover over the terror, and we fell in with this idea that everything was so marvellous—as it was.

BANET: It was easy to forget the terror . . .

BION: Yes . . . we just forgot it. A friend of mine went down to Manchester, and when he returned he said, "You know, the university is like a nightmare in reverse. You have no conception whatsoever of the state of affairs in Manchester: the misery, the unemployment, the total conditions. I walk in here—the rowing, the excitement, the races—and it's like coming into an utterly and totally unreal world of happiness, pleasantness, comfort—whereas when we go to Manchester we walk straight into this frightful state, which is actually the real one."

BANET: Margaret Rioch, in one of her comments on the Tavistock model, points out its strong emphasis on the tragic aspects, the seriousness of life. Your story sounds like the same thing—that behind all this idyllic university scene you were being reminded by your friend that there were serious conditions in Manchester—world events that were causing people pain.

BION: I don't think it is very unusual that one covers pain over with something that isn't tragic. If it's a nice day, you're jolly thankful it's a nice day; if I think back about England now, I always think of the weather as sunny. You just forget those vast spaces of time in which the fields are under water and that the springtime is cold and miserable and beastly. All you remember are the summer days—the summer weather and the summer conditions. You tend to concentrate on how magnificent everything is—how good life is—and to resent anybody who reminds you that, for most people, it isn't. Of course, nearly everybody learns the same trick—pretending to be more happy or fortunate than he actually is. Then you are taken by surprise if you happen to be taken ill. The illness itself is treated as if it were a fluke. I think that the more correct statement would be that the health of the individual is a fluke. For some reason, we've got this kind of apparatus up here in our heads which enables us to believe that good health—the kind of health you have at age thirty—is normal.

BANET: That viewpoint seems very much opposed to the human potential movement—the celebration of individuality, the talk about joy, about community. I'd be interested in how you view contemporary group movements that emphasize fulfilment and happiness.

BION: I don't really know enough about any of these other movements to be able to say anything particularly knowledgeable about them, but I do know about psychoanalysis. Psychoanalysis is based on the premise that it is abnormal to be unhappy—to be anxious— but it seems to me that as one goes into the business of dealing with others, it's a very questionable premise indeed. The usual part of life is involved with tragedy, sadness and decaying health. After all, one's health decays from the moment of birth, and there are people who have never been well; in some ways I think that they could be saner than people like myself who've had good health and who have been good athletes. A healthy person just doesn't appreciate why on earth he should have anything else but health. I don't know how to rate the baselines, but perhaps we should consider that suffering and rivalries with other human beings are really the normal standard. The poor, those who are less well-off, or the unhappy would naturally covet the riches, the wealth and the comfort of those who are well-off. This would apply to nations just as much as to individuals. It might be quite reasonable to suppose that the natural thing would be for wealthy and successful nations or individuals to find that they are the target of hostility.

BANET: It was, I think, Melanie Klein who stimulated your interest in psychoanalysis.

BION: Yes, Melanie Klein has certainly influenced me. Before that, John Rickman, whom I liked very much, was also very influential, although it was clear later on that he had various personal difficulties. We have to use people who have these difficulties. They are the people who become our teachers; they are the people who make the advances. I certainly remember him with a great deal of affection.

BANET: Was he at the Tavistock Institute?

BION: No. He was at the Institute of Psychoanalysis, but he was one of these "heretics" who had dealings with the Tavistock Institute, which was really considered to be grossly improper by the psychoanalysts.

BANET: Were you a heretic, too, at the Tavistock?

BION: Yes, I was. But I was also a heretic in the other direction because, although a member of the Tavistock Institute, I made contact with psychoanalysis and wanted to be, and did become, a psychoanalyst. In those days the British Institute of Psychoanalysis was afraid of appearing to condone activities that were not psychoanalytic by cooperating with the Tavistock Institute. It is not unlike the situation in the United States when American psychoanalysts think that psychoanalysis will be undermined by sanctioning psychoanalysts who support the theories of Melanie Klein.

I think the Tavistock Institute was then afraid that the freedom of thought, supposed to be the hallmark of the Institute, would be endangered by the bigotry and rigidity of the psychoanalysts. Therefore, any interchange between Rickman and members of the Tavistock was regarded with suspicion by both parties.

BANET: A. K. Rice is often regarded as a primary pupil of yours. Do you see him extending the theory?

BION: I don't really know enough of what he did. I was present with him only once at Amherst, when he took a small group (he didn't take the whole group), so I didn't really have a chance to get up to date with what he was doing. He happened also to be very ill, although I didn't know it at the time.

BANET: Your group theory emphasizes that a basic assumption of life exists below the surface of the group's work life. I'd like to hear your comments on how this operates in groups.

BION: Both words—basic and assumption—are important. It seems to me that it is not simply the assumption that is basic, but also that the thing that one's trying to talk about is basic. The difficulty is to know how to define or to detect this basic theory. You try to talk in as polite and civilized a manner as possible, but in the secrecy of your own mind, if you think of it, you're awakened by reality as you are jolted awake by an alarm clock. What language do you use about your alarm clock? How does language connect the basic, secret fantasy aspects of your mind with the realities of the outside world? In groups, you have the opportunity to hear language that attempts to express these basic assumptions. Indeed, one of the points about groups is that they provide an opportunity to see things collectively. Instead of a line of thirty people, one after the other, you see the whole collection of thirty people together. I think the group is a distortion, but so is a survey map—where you portray mountains and valleys on a flat surface by using contour lines. The group approach ought to have its own methods of portraying its basic assumption of life. What that method is is yet to be discovered, but it needs to be something that jams a whole lot of data together to portray the results on a flat surface.

BANET: Many people regard the notion of "basic assumptions" in groups as the key to understanding group process. But you're saying that the method to use that key needs to be elaborated.

BION: Yes, I think the notion of "basic assumption" needs tremendous investigation. For example, we all know people with rheumatic pains. An ordinary general practitioner in England knows of people who have been bedridden twenty or thirty years. Cancer gets all the publicity because nobody can be bothered with a subject like rheumatic complaints that is boring and tiresome and won't go away. I think that this is the direction in which the investigation of groups could go. If you could persuade thirty people with rheumatic pains to meet together, you would learn something. You would have to have a group expert, because I don't think that you could possibly keep a collection of people like that together—they would hate each other so much. They'd dare to come once, but then they would find that somebody else was occupying the stage, and they could never get a real chance to say how terrible their pains were. I think that only a group expert could stand it, and if he could, then I think something would emerge from that pattern that couldn't emerge if the expert saw those thirty people individually. I think that you can look at a group like a real cartographic map. The group theorist can learn to "read" the group.

BANET: In your book you use the analogy of a clock. It is possible to understand the individual parts of a clock, but you would not necessarily know that their function was to tell time until they all came together.

BION: It's true. It's like the process of a group. It's more than likely that the group process will tell you all about something that your innards could tell you—such as hunger—something you don't know cognitively. I think that the person who takes a group, the group specialist as it were, should be able to detect a pattern that may not be obvious to the rest of the group.

BANET: I associate that expression—"taking the group"—with you. Other people speak of "doing" groups or "leading" groups, and it is very clear in your writing that you "take" a group. You are observing something that you didn't create.

BION: One should always remember that, in fact, every member of a group "takes" a group if one could only see it in that way. The fellow who sits there and doesn't say a word from start to finish "takes" the group and exerts an influence on it. Sooner or later, somebody will notice: "You haven't said anything." Then he might ask, "If you come here week after week and don't say a word, what are we supposed to do?" But it is obvious that this person is in his own way taking a group—and yet he can say, "I've done nothing."

BANET: I have worked with groups in many different ways. When I am more personal and inviting, I'm pretty calm inside. But whenever I consult with a group in the Tavistock manner, I am frightened, especially at the beginning. It seems ominous—that perhaps something terrible will happen. It seems that in such a group there's always potential for terrible things happening.

BION: In psychoanalysis, when approaching the unconscious—that is, what we do not know—we, patient and analyst alike, are certain to be disturbed. In every consulting-room, there ought to be two rather frightened people: the patient and the psychoanalyst. If they are not both frightened, one wonders why they are bothering to find out what everyone knows.

I sometimes think that an analyst's feelings while taking a group—feelings while absorbing the basic assumptions of the group—are one of the few bits of what scientists might call evidence, because he can know what he is feeling. I attach great importance to feelings for that reason. You as an analyst can see for yourself what a shocking, poverty-stricken vocabulary it is for you—I'm frightened, I feel sexual, I feel hostile—and that's about it. But that's not what it's like in real life. In real life you have an orchestra: continuous movement and the constant slither of one feeling into another. You have to have a method to capture all that richness. In a group, you are in the unfortunate position of having very little evidence. The physician, the physical person, can get physical evidence, or so he thinks, anyway. When dealing with physical things, you can touch, you can feel, and you can smell, but we who use our minds are really up against it, because we don't know what the mind really is capable of perceiving. Even senses that were available to us at some stage in life we have lost.

Some sea creatures retain incredible sense perception. Take the mackerel. Its sense of smell is long range, so it can collect food because it can smell decaying matter, whatever it is, wherever it is, and can close in on it. Our own sense of smell seems to have deteriorated very considerably, and in fact, in order to get any kind of acute smell, you have to live in a watery element.

When human beings are born, they change from a watery fluid to a gaseous fluid—the air. The person takes some kind of fluid with him in the form of mucus; the nose can still operate but on a greatly diminished level. Of course, if there is too much of it, then we have what we call a catarrh and the watery element drowns our sense of smell.

BANET: So the person who takes a group is sniffing out or relying on some special sense.

BION: Well, I think it would be very wise to suppose so, and it might be possible to get more and more conscious of what this special sense is. Suppose you were observing a group of—say— Russians. You might say, "These Russians—they never smile, they never laugh." Well, if you're used to using these small muscles here around your mouth then you certainly notice it when another person doesn't use them. It may take you some time until you realize that they don't use their small muscles for smiling but they use something else—their feet or something (they may be dancers)—and express a smile in that way.

BANET: A fantasy I had travelling here to meet you was that you would look like Basil Rathbone dressed as Sherlock Holmes—a detective, constantly alert to every minor cue. It sounds like the group consultant is a detective, skilled at being attentive to nuances.

BION: Well, I think it is important to be able to develop that skill—to be able to sort out the information. Take a room like this. You can be aware of it, and if you're very observant you can have a pretty good memory of the things that are in the room. When you have masses of data, you can even say, "I went to their room, and I don't think that they are particularly aesthetic people." Well, that's an interpretation of these material objects. You've got to be a gatherer of your sense impressions, but it is fatal if you allow yourself to be drowned in impressions—so much mucus, so to speak, that you can't even smell—so that instead of your perception being an advantage, it becomes a liability. I think that this is the complaint that so many Frenchmen feel about Victor Hugo. When André Gide was asked who was his country's greatest poet, he said, "Victor Hugo, alas." Well, it's incredible—Hugo's observations; they're really extraordinary. The visual images he's able to carry off are impressive, but you don't get the impression of Hugo as a great thinker, because he doesn't seem to synthesize it. It leaves the reader to synthesize his observations.

BANET: That would be one function of theory—to provide that synthesis of impressions. I would like to hear you talk about large groups—institutions and organizations.

BION: Institutions and organizations are all the same—they're dead. Let me put it this way. An institution behaves in accordance with certain laws and bylaws—it has to make them—and all organizational laws become as rigid and definitive as the laws of physics. An organization becomes hard and inanimate like this table.

I don't know of anyone who can say at what point animate changes into inanimate. Take, for example, a dung heap. It seems inanimate, and then maggots appear, and it becomes animate. The trouble about all institutions—the Tavistock Institute and every one that we have—is that they are dead, but the people inside them aren't, and the people grow, and something's going to happen. What usually happens is that the institutions (societies, nations, states and so forth) make laws. The original laws constitute a shell, and then new laws expand that shell. If it were a material prison, you could hope that the prison walls would be elastic in some sort of way. If organizations don't do that, they develop a hard shell, and then expansion can't occur because the organization has locked itself in.

BANET: Currently, there's a lot of interest in trying to get organizations to be more responsive to human needs. Does that have some chance for success?

Bion: If the organization does not respond to human needs, either it or the individual will be destroyed. It's like an animal that protects itself by growing a hard shell. What's going to happen when the animal grows? What's going to happen to either the shell or the animal? The ordinary bird has sense enough to crack the shell and walk out.

The curious thing is that the mind itself seems to be able to produce a shell of its own. People say things like "I don't want to hear any more of these new ideas. I've been very happy. I don't want to have my ideas upset. If you start making me think of this and that, well then, I might have to bother about the troubles of Los Angeles. Why can't I live here in peace and quiet?" I think there is always a resistance to development and change and a tendency to think what a horrible thing this maggot is that tries to animate the dung heap.

BANET: Institutions that have been around for some time, like the United States or the Catholic Church, profess an interest in renewal and changing, but then it seems like perverse things happen. Either the leaders are removed or people become very pessimistic about the possibility of change.

Bion: I've often thought that the United States has an intellectual belief in itself as the "top" nation. There is a feeling, therefore, that the institutions that are all very well for an unimportant or beginning nation are no good at all to one on the top. I think that there will be a tendency to rebel against this restraining force, this invisible shell, which is so difficult to imagine—even to conceive of at all.

One just does not know what the restraints on a nation are. In the early stages, they were fairly clear. It was quite easy for Americans to see the British as the restraining force and to rebel against that. But then, this newly formed institution started growing a shell again. Its new laws and Constitution were enshrined. Now a feeling has developed that the Constitution—which is the mental shell of the United States—isn't really adequate for the world as it is, because the nation is growing and is aware, therefore, of the pressure and the hostility that come from outside. The people of the United States may want to live in peace; they may not want to attack anybody; but then they find that they have to have a navy; they have to have an air force; they have to have an army—all of which they may hate having. Once again, a shell within a shell starts growing. They have to have a secret service. Then suppose they feel that the secret service and the police want to know what they're up to, but they don't see that it is anyone else's business. So they can be aware of the very shell that they're growing while it is growing. That is obviously a most uncomfortable proceeding, because you can hate the shell and yet believe that it is necessary. For example, I don't want to be invaded by some foreign country. All right, then I'll put up with the army, navy and air force, but then the army, navy and air force say they want me as a recruit and I must learn how to bear arms. I hate the shell but come to see it as necessary.

BANET: At the time of the political assassinations there was a lot of editorial comment to the effect that "we are all guilty", that an assassin has some valence with the rest of society—he acts for all of us.

Bion: I think that one needs to beware because that judgement can be made too prematurely and precociously. If one judges prematurely, then he clamps down on it—adds another shell. I can see this with myself. The more tired I am, the more quickly I give interpretations. It's such a frightful business to retain your freshness of mind; the mind goes on working even though you don't have the foggiest idea what's going on.

That's why one tries to learn and take some sort of scientific, religious or artistic approach to the problem of history—it's simply difficult to visualize what on earth the problem is in this country. One can only get these somewhat trivial models that one picks up from the past.

BANET: I know that you are concentrating on individual psychoanalysis, rather than on groups, and that you have written recently on the problem of knowledge and perception. What is exciting for you these days?

BION: I'm working mostly with individuals now. The investigation of the individual still has a lot to yield. The advantage of the group is that you can see certain elements much more easily. With the individual, you may find it very difficult to see disturbance; the patient is so rational, so calm, so all right, that you are misled by this surface appearance. As Virgil described it in the *Aeneid*, Palinurus, although tempted by the God of Sleep, is not taken in by the deceptively calm and beautiful exterior. When the analyst allows himself to be deceived, he will say, "Well, this patient has never had any troubles, has never been any trouble, always got on well, is loved and liked by all of us, and is a very affectionate and charming person. I can't understand how or why he should commit suicide." That, of course, is a very dramatic thing—when a person brings his life to an end without anybody having observed what was going on. To see what's inside—that's the difficulty.

I am interested in the individual—in his struggle against the pressure from the shells built around him. We talked about the shells of organizations earlier. Well, individuals have shells too. When you are dealing with a mind, or a personality, then you get these same shell-building processes, but they're much more difficult to deal with because you can't fall back on physical observation. Perhaps if you were more sensitive, or you employed more sensitive instruments, you could do it, but not as things are at present.

If you have an active mind, it is pressing against the obstacles and restraints to its operation, and every activity, or your own personal fatigue, puts a restraint on you, so you can't even locate the shell. The inhibition of one's self produces difficulties. It would be so simple if one could say, "Oh well, you're suffering from these inhibitions, and we all know what Freud said about inhibitions." But that isn't all there is to say about inhibitions. We have this vast universe and we have various objects scattered about, but the outside world is out of our control. It is simply out there. However, we have some choice about what to pay attention to. This means that I have to split things up—table, lamp, and so on. If you think of it in slow motion, you have to choose the order of precedence. So when you choose to try to get out of your inhibitions and restraints you are up against a problem of splitting things up—calling this object a book and saying this is a table. I don't know that that would be agreed to by the person who has concentrated on the atomic constitution of the thing, because where should the table end? Where can you say on the one side is a table and on the other side is air?

BANET: Well, it seems that I might come up with a practical solution. I might believe that the table is really a collection of molecules, but I expect something to rest on it if I put it there.

BION: That's the point. One has to come to a practical decision; at some point we have to translate our thoughts and ideas into action, and, so far, we've been able to do that.

BANET: I'm interested in your thinking about the growing interest in Eastern philosophies in this country, It seems that we're departing from Western European traditions and adopting Eastern perspectives.

BION: I don't think that we can depart from the Western European tradition, but what is so striking is that we've become aware that there *are* different methods of thinking. I don't know Sanscrit (I'm no good at languages at all), but as far as I can tell by translations, there is a most striking resemblance, say, between the *Baghavad*

Gita and Meister Eckhart—a resemblance between entirely differ-ent religions. Both of them are surrounded by this type of think-ing—breaking out of one's shell—and it upsets a great many people. The *Baghavad Gita* is still read after hundreds of years.

BANET: Eastern and Western mystical thought both suggest a re-duction or destruction of the ego—that you can, in some way, break out of the shell of self.

BION: Freud made a very illuminating observation about the ego, the id and the superego. It's only when one tries to contemplate it, tries to look at the human being, that he begins to see that these psychodynamic formulations, which are very fruitful, are really not quite good enough. But it's difficult, because one doesn't really know whether one's misrepresenting Freud or whether one's got onto the right track.

It seems to me that one could say that the mind has a kind of skin that is in contact with somebody else. For example, we are talking together. Why? How? I may quite mistakenly think I know what you're asking me and what you're telling me, but why? What are these senses? If it is a question of my sense of touch, I can say that it's the skin. But what is this mental skin that enables two people to be (although it is a metaphorical use of the term) in "contact"? We borrow the term from the physical world, but it isn't touching. One can feel it; he can bring his mind (as Dr. Johnson says) up against the other person, and he can be aware of a con-tact—something that he just has—with another. You have to use some words if you want to talk about it at all. This contact requires labelling.

BANET: I'm certainly aware when I'm not in contact with someone.

BION: But it is very difficult to know why we know that.

BANET: The philosophical aspects of your work are really where a lot of your attention is. I can see you playing with concepts—putting things together. I'm interested in hearing more about that.

BION: I'm not sure that I can find the passage. In the *Phaedrus*, Socrates points out that language is extremely ambiguous, and therefore difficulties are produced when you have to turn your thoughts into action, which is unambiguous. The two of us (two entities, characters or personalities) meet—what are we to do? Usually it isn't an acute enough problem to be noticeable, because an attempt can be made to talk the same language. But supposing one found himself on a desert island with someone he'd never met and whose language he didn't know—what way would he bridge the gap? Sign languages are commonplace, but nobody has really studied how, in fact, contact is made.

BANET: I would put my money on some kind of collaborative action or work.

BION: That's the important thing about the group approaches—it may be possible to detect what this work of making contact is. The group has to find some way in which it can meet again—some method of communication between the various members who are physically discrete, different people. It seems that you end where your body ends, but it's a very puzzling situation. People can meet and talk and extend themselves into one another. There even seems to be a kind of communicating that extends over the centuries between Plato and the *Gita* and Meister Eckhart and us.

BANET: Religion has some explanation for that—the spirit.

BION: Because religious people have been at it a long time, they have a considerable vocabulary, although we could say that it isn't adequate. You'd have to invent some sort of extension; you'd have to burst out somewhere. To me it appears that you would have to have this little pimple that you call psychoanalysis appearing at the surface. The trouble is that we are so limited—we analysts think that if we are a part of the pimple the rest of the body doesn't exist—that the religious world (whatever it is) has ceased to exist. Psychoanalysts have been particularly blind to the topic of religion. If we try to extend—if we happen to be at the edge of the growing point—it's absurd to imagine that there isn't anything behind that or that there isn't anything that we're pushing against.

This brings us to another point. If psychoanalysis is a kind of extension of the religious world, then the religious world would object to that extension. The Jew might wonder about this distortion of the Hebrew tradition called Christianity. You get the same thing over and over again. What are these newfangled ideas—psychoanalysis, psychology, groups, therapy? They're all fallacious. "All this has been known by the church for hundreds of years" would be a common reply. Alternatively, "This is dangerous and heretical. You'll destroy religion if you start introducing sex into things."

BANET: It seems that at a later stage the church somewhat embraces psychoanalysis and incorporates it into its training.

BION: Yes, but it does seem to be the same process of getting a sufficient shell to be protected and then having to rebel against a shell because it not only protects you, but also can shut you up. The shell that protects also kills. Let me put it this way: individuals can be so rigid that they don't seem to have any ideas or they can be so free and so profuse in their outpourings of ideas that it really amounts to a pathological condition. But the same things seem to me to apply to the state or to any organization. People can't just easily escape and take up a new mission and still maintain that they're members of your organization. On the other hand, people outside shouldn't be allowed to say they are members of your organization and use you in order to gain a sort of cloak of respectability for their ideas. So there's the problem. How permeable are you to make this envelope of self, this shell? Or to get back to the Freudian phrase, how permeable is the ego to be? There are pressures from inside and, on the other hand, pressures from without. To what extent is one to allow any idea to come in? One feels that there's a need for a sort of discriminating screen. If it were physical, one could try to invent some sort of sieve that sieves off what one doesn't want and allows in what one does want in. When it's the mind, I don't know how it could be done.

BANET: It sounds like you're regarding your work, especially your book *Experiences in Groups*, as just a beginning. Many other people regard it as a definitive piece of work.

BION: That would be a great pity. The book is not the final view, and I urge people working with groups to make it out of date as soon as possible.

BANET: I have a feeling it's going to be a while before it's out of date.

BION: I am sure certain basic things in *Experiences in Groups* are worth retaining. I hope that is true; otherwise, we could be leading people up the garden path. I hope that there are certain things that are still operative, but to allow "Bion's theory" to operate in a rigid way such as print would be ridiculous, because that puts a restraint on the growth of the individual and the individuals who make a group.

BANET: In the past few years, the A. K. Rice Institute and its centres have become more popular; there are more people going to group relations conferences and learning about groups and your theory. Is that gratifying to you?

BION: It doesn't make much difference for me, in one sense, because I'm out of group work and I'm still working on individuals very much; but I certainly think the work of the Institute is very important. But, again, the Rice Institute must realize that it is not going to be exempted from the problems that confront the great organizations like the United States or the individual states.

BANET: It's subject to the same problems.

BION: The same problems . . . You've got to have these rules—these bylaws. Of course, one can make new laws so there's got to be a certain flexibility, but, unfortunately for organizations and institutes, it's difficult to be flexible.

BANET: Are you going to write some more about groups?

BION: I hope so, but, you know, one of the difficulties today is finding the time. At present, I am heavily committed to my work with individuals.

INDEX